ENDORSEMENTS

John Maisel is a gifted evangelist who is "ready in season and out of season" to give the gospel. He has dedicated his life to godly principles and he's laid them out in his book. If you're looking for the simple truth of Jesus, this book will help you find it.

— Coach Joe Gibbs
Founder and Chairman of Joe Gibbs Racing Team

The title of the book is very fitting for John Maisel. He has known for over fifty years that God loves him and as he lives his life, you know for certain whom he trusts. Find a quiet place, pick up the book and enjoy!

— Norm Miller
Chairman of the Board, Interstate Batteries

John Maisel has ministered around the world in his lifetime. He has heard the longing of the human heart. In writing this book he has captured the heart of Jesus, who knows our needs better than we do. It is through our submission to trust Him that we find out just how much He loves us and how much He cares. Whether you are a young believer, a weathered follower, male or female, this book is for you. I had to put it down many times to just digest the wisdom John imparts.

— Sally Meredith
Cofounder of Christian Family Life with husband Don Meredith

John Maisel is the most courageous ambassador for Christ I have ever known. God has made him an Isaiah for our day, pointing the world to Jesus with boldness and grace. As you listen to his story and feel his heart, the Spirit will use his words to inflame your passion for the King.

— Jim Denison
Denison Forum on Truth and Culture

Many people "talk." Some people, like John Maisel, actually "walk the talk." Personally, John's "walk" makes me want the relationship he has with Jesus. John's "talk"—powerfully conveyed in this book—frees us from the unbearable burden of performance. . .and positions us to receive God's priceless love.

— June Hunt
Founder, CEO, CSO (Chief Servant Officer), Hope for the Heart
Author, How to Forgive. . .When You Don't Feel Like It

It is with great joy that I recommend this book by my longtime friend and ministry partner, John Maisel. You never have to guess what John stands for. He always takes people back to Jesus and to the grace that is found in Him. In this new work, John tells story after story of how God's grace has shown up for him personally, causing his heart to cling to God's love with childlike faith. By relating these personal accounts, John inspires all of us to abandon ourselves to God's sovereign will and perfect love, so as to live boldly with joy and confidence as we abandon ourselves to follow Him.

— **Hugh O. Maclellan, Jr.**
Executive Chairman of the Board
The Maclellan Foundation, Inc.

Having ministered side-by-side with John Maisel for over twenty years, I've long known how exciting it is to work with a true hero of the faith. As his successor in the role of President of East–West Ministries, I am learning how incredibly humbling it is to follow in his footsteps. When you read this book you'll appreciate why John feels the grip of God's grace as intensely—and intentionally—as anyone I know. Time and again you'll find yourself saying, "That's the sort of walk with God that I want to have." But you'll also be challenged to "live dangerously" for God in a world where most people are "playing it safe." So be forewarned: John would have us place such tenacious trust in God's perfect love that we laugh in the face of risk and sacrifice for the glory of the Name of Jesus in this dark world and even find ourselves willing to risk our very lives for His cause as we weep over the eternal destiny of others that do not yet know Him.

— **Kurt Nelson**
President/CEO
East–West Ministries International

RADICAL TRUST

RADICAL TRUST

THE TWO MOST IMPORTANT TRUTHS
JESUS WANTS YOU TO KNOW.

JOHN MAISEL

FOREWORD
DR. HOWARD G. HENDRICKS
DISTINGUISHED PROFESSOR EMERITUS, DALLAS THEOLOGICAL SEMINARY

Library of Congress Cataloging-in-Publication Data
Pending

Printed in the U.S.
14 13 12 11 10 09 08
7 6 5 4 3 2 1

SPECIAL THANKS

To my wife, Susie, who has been at the forefront of my learning about God's grace by giving me a great deal of undeserved love.

To A'Dina and Harry Smith, my daughter and son-in-law, who have been my greatest encouragers.

To Nicole and Maxson, my grandchildren, who continue to teach me much about Jesus and how to follow Him in childlike faith.

ACKNOWLEDGMENTS

To all the East–West Ministries staff, Board, and friends who continue
to keep the focus of getting the Good News of Christ's
love to the four corners of the globe.

Special thanks to Bill Hendricks for helping to organize and
edit this manuscript over the last year.

All financial proceeds will go to East–West Ministries International to
help advance the gospel to the least reached areas of the globe.

CONTENTS

FOREWORD

As he stood in my office, he was every inch a he–man. His words, his posture, his confidence—all denoted the former Marine officer that he was. Yet something else radiated from him, as well: an intensity, a vigor that propelled his entire manner. Here was a man of purpose, en route to. . .? Well, he was asking me.

John Maisel had sloshed through the brambles of Nam to engage the enemies of freedom. But he'd also confronted a force far more powerful than any gun-toting human. He had caught a vision of God, and his heart was on fire. I felt the heat and saw the sparkle. Here was a man on the move!

Nonetheless, John had learned to stop and get his spiritual bearings so as to move in step with the Spirit of Christ. As we talked about his future, I could hear a faint echo in my mind of Jim Elliot. Jim had been assigned to me as my "little brother" when I was a senior at Wheaton College. He became one of the legendary martyrs who gave their lives for the testimony of the gospel a half century ago on the sandy shores of the Curaray River in remote Ecuador. Jim's famous quotation still rings in my ears: "He is no fool who gives what he cannot keep to gain what he cannot lose." John seemed to possess that same spiritual maturity far beyond his years.

It is now more than six decades since I began teaching would-be vocational Christian ministers. Very few young men have crossed my path with as much eagerness as John did. Like a diver on the high board, he plunged into the world of Christian leadership, honed his business skills, sharpened his theological acumen, and like an Olympic torchbearer, began traveling the world to bring light into the darkness of sin-shuttered hearts.

RADICAL TRUST

From the battlefield to the college campus to the offices of a ruthless financial world, wherever he goes, John marches on with purpose. He reminds me of the biblical Caleb who, in his ninth decade of life and infused with the passion of Moses, his mentor, cried out to the field commander, Joshua, "Give me this mountain!" In a similar way, John never stops reaching out for the next challenge.

Radical Trust invites readers to journey alongside this remarkable man on his varied path, and hopefully to breathe in something of his exhilaration. Flight-tested in the real world of what Shakespeare called "sharp-toothed unkindness," John's message uncovers the essence of winning in life and in death. How does masculine virility square with trust and love? Therein lies the secret of John Maisel's competence and potency. It's not really about John at all. This book guides the reader into a treasure trove of truth unlike any to be found elsewhere.

Howard G. Hendricks
Distinguished Professor Emeritus
Leadership and Christian Education
Dallas, Texas

Chapter 1

IS THERE MORE TO THE CHRISTIAN LIFE?

"Why should we hear the gospel twice when there are millions who have never heard it even once in their life?" — Hudson Taylor

I was sitting in the lobby of the Hotel National, waiting for my taxi to the airport. The Hotel National has always been one of Moscow's centers of prestige and power. From the day it opened in 1903, it began attracting the big shots: politicians, dignitaries, diplomats, royalty, business tycoons, celebrities, and the like. When Lenin and the Bolsheviks took over in 1917, they claimed it for their headquarters. Later, in the 1930s, the hotel was updated with spoils from palaces and estates of the former elite—opulent pieces of furniture, masterful works of art, fine paintings, and rare antiques.

RADICAL TRUST

I almost always stayed at the National when I traveled to Moscow in the 1980s, which was often. I liked it there, not because of the luxury and finery—that was certainly nice—but because an international hotel was safer. I was, after all, at the very heart of Soviet Russia. Indeed, there was a great view of the Kremlin from the hotel. But in a place frequented by foreigners, I was less likely to attract attention.

So as I was sitting there with time on my hands, a couple of guys walked into the lobby. They sat down nearby and started a conversation. One of them looked to be an African. But what really caught my attention was they were both speaking English.

Let me tell you, when you've been traveling in a foreign country for several days or weeks, your ears can get tired of hearing languages you don't understand. And even when someone addresses you in English, their English typically has a foreign accent to it. So when someone starts speaking clearly and articulately in Western–style English, that grabs your attention.

Besides, I'm just naturally curious about people. About who they are, what their story is, what they think, what they believe. Especially what they believe about God and about His Son, Jesus.

You see, my reason for traveling to the Soviet Union was to talk to people about Jesus. Many of the people I'd meet had never heard the truths about Jesus. I was the first person who had ever told them who He is. Others had heard about Jesus and became His followers. But for obvious reasons, they had to keep their faith secret. I had the privilege of meeting with them in secret to celebrate our common bond in Christ while encouraging them with prayer and basic Bible teaching.

Divine Appointments

I operated on the belief that every person who came across my path was a divine appointment. Truly, God had brought us together for a purpose. Quite often, the intended purpose was for me to tell that person what I knew about Jesus—if they were interested.

So it was with the English-speaking man from Africa. He and the other fellow had finished their conversation, and now he was sitting by himself. Probably waiting for a ride, just like I was.

A little conversation started up in my head—a conversation that happens a lot for me because of my belief in divine appointments: *Do I say something to him?* Pause. *Maybe I shouldn't say anything.* Pause. *But I really ought to at least see if he's interested.* Pause. *No, what if he's not.* Pause. *I don't want to offend him.* Pause.

Perhaps you've had a similar conversation with yourself when an opportunity comes along to discuss spiritual things. I find a lot of us Christians have little lists we go through for all the reasons why we should keep quiet when the Lord is in fact prompting us to reach out to somebody.

Finally, I just turned to the guy and said, "I noticed you were speaking English."

He smiled and replied, "Yes."

I said, "Do you mind if I ask you a question?"

He said, "No, feel free."

So I said, "Do you have any interest in spiritual things? Or do you ever think much about the existence of God?"

Now I have to admit, these questions are not the sort most people are used to hearing. But then, that's the point. Most people get asked chitchat questions about what they do for work, or where they're from, or what they think of the weather. Those topics are fine. But rarely does anyone ask a person about what is going on inside of them—especially as it relates to what God might be doing in his or her heart.

I've discovered no matter what things look like on the surface, no matter how strong or "together" or self-satisfied an individual may appear, or no matter how angry or hostile they may seem toward God, the Lord is at work behind the scenes in that person's life. If I will trust that, then when I ask people if they would like to talk about spiritual matters, more often than not they would. But usually they don't talk about such things, because no one has bothered to open a door for them to speak about spiritual matters.

RADICAL TRUST

This man turned out to be interested. For a moment he just looked at me. And for a moment I wondered if maybe my fear of offending him had come true. But suddenly he blurted out, "If you had asked me that question two weeks ago, I would have said no. But today, I'm interested."

With such an opening, I leaned forward and introduced myself. Soon we were deep in conversation. I learned he was from Ethiopia. He was working for the government. He was very intelligent, And, he asked great questions. I never found out what had happened during the previous two weeks that made him interested now in talking about God. But that didn't matter.

To make a long story short, after about an hour's conversation, I had an opportunity to explain the gospel to him. I showed him from the Bible how Jesus had come to be his Savior. I told him he needed to trust in what Jesus did on the cross to take away his sin.

After making sure he understood the gospel message, the man finally said to me, "I want to make that decision." And so we prayed together, right there in the lobby of the hotel. He told Jesus he wanted forgiveness for his sins, and from that point on he was going to be a follower of Jesus.

Just then, my taxi arrived. I hated to break off the conversation. But I really had to go. So I scribbled down my name and contact information and gave it to him. And then I left.

I never saw my new brother in Christ again.

Chapter **2**

"I MUST TELL OTHERS!"

"If Jesus Christ be God and died for me, then no sacrifice can be too great for me to make for Him." — C. T. Studd

Even though I never saw the man from Ethiopia again, I did hear from him. About four or five months after our encounter in Moscow, I received a letter from him. He told me he was writing from prison. The authorities had imprisoned him because of his Christian faith.

To give some background: when Emperor Haile Selassie was deposed as the leader of Ethiopia in 1974, the government degenerated into a series of coups and uprisings lasting for twenty years. Marxism gained a strong foothold, and hundreds of thousands were killed in various acts of terror and genocide. The country plunged in political chaos. Worse, it was in a spiritual death spiral.

This man returned to this grim political climate. He knew the Ethiopian authorities hated Jesus. He knew they would probably hate him for receiving Jesus as Savior. Nevertheless, when he returned home, he couldn't stop talking about Jesus. He wanted everyone to know there really is a God. And, He's a God of incredible love. This loving God has made a way for people to know Him, and the only way is through Jesus. Talking about this good news was something he just had to do. It was not something he had to "try" to do. It was something he could not help from doing. He wanted everyone he knew to hear the same gospel message he had heard from me during our "chance" encounter in Russia.

So it was only a matter of time before he was arrested and put in prison. In his letter, he gave me the address of his family and asked if I would contact them to let them know what had happened to him. Of course I followed through with his request. Also, I kept him in my prayers. Beyond praying for him, there was nothing else I could do.

A while later, I heard from him again. He informed me that he might be getting out of prison soon. At least, he thought that was a possibility. But what he most wanted was for me to send him more information about the Christian life and what it means to follow Jesus. I put together a package of materials and mailed it off to him. But after sending the requested materials, I never heard from him again.

Now I don't know what thoughts and feelings come to you as I relate this story, which happened thirty years ago. Perhaps, if you're a Christian from America, the story causes you to admire this man's boldness, courage, and commitment. You might describe him as someone of unusual faith.

But here's what's remarkable: The man's faith was by no means unusual. Bold faith like that was the norm for the people I met who started following Jesus in those Iron Curtain days. Almost without exception, from the moment they trusted Christ, their immediate response was, "I've got to go tell my friends about this." This kind of reaction happened consistently—I'd say almost every time. Whether it was a person I might have met on the street, or a professor in a university, or someone like a waiter or a cab driver or a salesclerk, it was always the same pattern: within an hour or two of making their decision for Christ, the person invariably had the impulse to say something like, "I've got many friends who need to hear this message!"

I still see the same pattern today. Even in countries like Iran, Uzbekistan, Myanmar, certain districts in India, and other places where it is extremely dangerous to talk about Jesus. I'm sure new believers in those areas consider the risks of going public with their faith. But those risks don't seem to be a hindrance to them. It's as if they've had a spiritual DNA implanted into them compelling them to tell others about Jesus. Maybe they can't do it openly and freely. But even if they have to do it in a whisper, they can't resist telling people around them about the message of Jesus. Such a response is the norm for new Christians almost everywhere in the world—the only real exceptions being Western Europe (the former stronghold of Christianity) and the United States.

Saved, But Silent

In contrast, when I come home to the United States, I find Christians who are mostly silent when it comes to talking with people about Jesus. Does that not strike you as odd? Oh, yes, we have lots of churches in America. Hundreds of thousands of churches, in fact. We have freedom of religion. We also have freedom of speech. And we have Christian bookstores, Christian radio stations, Christian music, Christian blogs, Christian colleges, and Christian organizations. We have lots of Christian things because we've got a lot of Christians. But I don't hear many Christians talking to the people around them about Jesus.

I'm not the only one. Probe Ministries, in the Dallas suburb of Plano, partnered with Barna Research Group in December 2010 to conduct a statistically valid survey of 817 born-again Christians in the United States, entitled, "The Culturally Captive Christian Study 2010." For the purposes of research, Barna defines a "born-again Christian" as someone who answers "yes" to two statements: (1) "I have made a personal commitment to Jesus that is still important in my life today"; and (2) "I know I am going to heaven when I die because I confessed my sins and accepted Jesus as my Savior."

Among the questions these Christians were asked was: "Some people talk about traditional forms of spiritual engagement. What do you do, if anything, that you consider to be traditional spirituality, in a typical month?" A number of activities were listed, and survey participants were allowed to check as many of the activities as they wished. Only 1 percent selected "witness to others" as something they do in a typical month.

Wow! Only 1 percent. Why so low? What accounts for such a small number? And what accounts for the fact that so many Christians in the West tell me their experience as a believer is mediocre at best? The vast majority of them are good, churchgoing men and women. Nevertheless, person after person will express disappointment with how their walk with Christ is turning out. They are fully aware of Jesus' bold claim that He came to bring life, and an abundance of it (see John 10:10). But somehow that abundance of life has eluded them.

Likewise, they know about the fruit of the Spirit: love, joy, peace, patience, kindness, goodness, faithfulness, gentleness, self-control (Galatians 5:22–23). But they are compelled to admit they personally experience very little love, joy, peace, and so on.

In the end, they often ask me, "What's wrong, John? There must be more to the Christian life than what I'm experiencing."

What do I say to them?

Chapter 3

EXPERIENCING
GOD

"Expect great things from God. Attempt great things for God."
— William Carey

If you're among the millions of Christians in the United States wondering if there's more to life in Christ than what you're experiencing, I believe God shouts back: *Yes, My beloved, there is!* God intends so much more for His people!

So what's the problem? Well, no doubt many factors are at work. But if I had to boil it down to one main issue, it would be this: You cannot experience the fullness of Christ's life unless and until you are gripped by the depth of Christ's love—His love for you. Not just knowing about

His love. Not just talking about it. But personally **experiencing** His love for you.

It was for this very reason that Paul prayed some two thousand years ago on behalf of *all* believers, including you and me:

[I pray] that you, being rooted and grounded in love [that is, Christ's love for us], may be able to comprehend [to understand and believe so as to act on it] with all the saints [meaning, all of us who believe in Christ] what is the breadth and length and height and depth, and to know the love of Christ [not just know about it intellectually, but to personally experience Christ's love through believing] which surpasses knowledge [His love is reasonable and logical, but it goes beyond reason and logic into experience], that you may be filled up to all the fullness of God [experience the presence and power of God]. (Ephesians 3:17–19)

Take a moment to examine Paul's prayer carefully. Notice the heart of it is that God would empower us to know the love of Christ. **Not our love for Christ, but Christ's love for us.** Paul prays that we would "know" that love. Yet, he clearly states that Christ's love for us "surpasses knowledge." So intellect alone is not enough to fully grasp it. Yes, logic and reason play a role. But to "know" Christ's love in the sense Paul is describing it means to be affected by that love at the core of who we are. We give in to it, we respond to it, we feel it thrilling our hearts, we trust it, we rest in it.

In short, Paul is talking about an experiential knowledge. He is asking God to allow us to "comprehend" the incomprehensible love of Christ for us. To explore how vast that love is—how broad and long and high and deep it is.

What happens when people are overwhelmed by the enormity of Christ's love for them? They begin to trust that love and to live in ways God asks them to live. With the result that they become "filled up to all the fullness of God." In other words, they at last encounter the fullness of life Christ promised—the abundance of life for which so many Christians long.

So on the basis of Paul's prayer, I repeat my earlier assertion: We cannot experience the fullness of Christ's life unless and until we are gripped by the depth of Christ's love. Again, not our love for Christ, but Christ's love for us.

A Defining Premise

You see, there are two themes repeated throughout the Bible, which is where God has revealed Himself as the Source of true life. Again and again, He stresses two bedrock realities:

- The first is a *promise*: "I love you!"
- The second is an *invitation*: "Trust Me!"

I believe that life in Christ ebbs and flows around those two realities: "I love you! Trust Me!" If we embrace those two statements from God, we will experience a transformation of our lives. We will be able to live boldly, humbly, lovingly, and radically for the sake of Jesus Christ. We will move far beyond the impoverished notion that Jesus is just a ticket to heaven. We will experience nothing short of Jesus' power, here and now, to invigorate our souls, calm our anxieties, diminish our fears, and leverage our lives for His glory. Isn't that what we really long for—to live lives of eternal significance?

"I love you! Trust Me!" Those two statements from God Himself serve as the defining premise for our lifestyles with Christ on a daily basis. We could state it like this:

The depth of our willingness to surrender to Jesus is directly related to the depth of our belief that God really

11

loves us with perfect love. Only as we trust His love will we surrender to His authority and experience a relationship with God that becomes real and satisfying.

In the next section, I want to do what Paul encourages us to do: to explore the vast riches of Christ's love for us. Then, in the second section, we will consider how that love compels us to trust the God of love with our very lives.

"I LOVE YOU!"

PART I

Chapter 4

A NEW
RELATIONSHIP

"Without His Holy Spirit we are useless. We are like ships without wind, coals without fire, chariots without horses, and branches without sap. We are useless." — Charles Spurgeon

Like a lot of Americans, I grew up in a nominally Christian family. We attended a church where I heard about religion, but not much about the gospel. The basic message was, "Live a good life." Nothing wrong with such an outlook, except the church and I had really different ideas about what constituted a "good life." Let's just say on a scale of 1 to 10, I was on the wild side!

RADICAL TRUST

Then I went off to Oklahoma State University to play football. During my freshman year, I was invited to hear someone speak at a meeting. They talked about Jesus. They explained how Jesus had died on the cross for my sins. And, they said I could have a personal relationship with this same Jesus if I would trust Him and give my life to Him.

All of this was new news to me. I knew there was a God, but I didn't know diddly-squat about Him or about the Bible or spiritual things. Later in the night, it clicked for me what it meant to trust in Christ. So I did. And my life was radically changed.

Such new news was good news, but it was also bad news. The good news, of course, was I had a new relationship with God, through Christ. Fantastic! The bad news was word eventually got out the freshman quarterback had become a follower of Christ. When some of the Christian leaders on campus heard about it, they said, "Hey, let's get John to talk about his newfound faith." They started promoting me as someone to listen to in terms of knowing Christ. In fact, very quickly after I had received Christ, I found myself on television. I remember the interviewer asking, "So John, tell us about how you intend to reach the campus for Christ."

I was like, "Reach the campus?! Where did that come from?" I had no idea what the person was talking about. I was just a brand-new believer and fairly clueless as to what this Christian thing was all about. Who knows how I answered the question? I was just winging it.

Then someone asked me, "John, would you give your testimony to a sorority?" I didn't know what a "testimony" was. I'd never heard the term before! But I remembered from back in high school when the druggies who got out of prison would come to our youth groups and tell us about their conversions. They always had dramatic, life-and-death tales of sin and redemption, which held everyone's attention. So I thought, "I guess that's how you do it." I then made up a "testimony."

I must have done a great job, because all these women came up to me afterward, gushing with praise: "Oh, John, that was great!"

And I thought, *Oh, you like what I said? Well, let me see what else I can do to impress you.* I mean, this demonstrated how green I was when I first became a Christian. And yet, despite all of the initial silliness, I knew at the core of my being something had dramatically changed inside.

From the Heights to the Depths

And just like the brand-new believers behind the Iron Curtain whom I mentioned earlier, I quickly began to talk about Jesus with my teammates and the guys living in my dorm. It was just instinctive—I could not **not** talk about Jesus. I wanted everyone to know what I had discovered about Him.

So I was on somewhat of an emotional high for about eighteen to twenty months. This mind-set made me vulnerable for what happened next. Lacking any real leadership from a mature believer, and not knowing anything about how one grows in relation to Christ, the roots of my newfound faith had little to cling to other than the initial rush of getting saved. So my spiritual life began to wane. I enjoyed having people listen to my "testimony." And I got to where I was thinking, *Hey, I'm pretty good at this up-front thing.* Add to that the enormous ego boost of being an athlete—the starting quarterback, no less. It was very heady.

Except I still wanted to live the way I wanted to live—the way I'd lived in high school—the way most of my buddies at college were living. A tension point developed. Even I could see that doing wild stuff and playing the field were incompatible with going public with my faith in front of the team, fraternities, sororities, and other groups. So I had to sneak around, which of course meant living a double-life.

Fortunately, just as God had saved me from my sins, He also saved me from myself by taking me out of the game, so to speak. During my senior year in college, I signed on with the Houston Oilers (now the Tennessee Titans). Naturally I was elated for an opportunity to play professional football. I thought I had it made. And I believed I was the cream of the crop. This pride made me a prime target for God to get my attention. All of a sudden, just when I thought my future was set, I got cut from the team. Out of nowhere!

I still had a semester to go to obtain my degree, so I returned to school and graduated. Then, because I had signed up for ROTC (Reserve Officers' Training Corps) as a sophomore, and had a commission in the Marine Corps, I reported for duty. I was immediately sent to officers' school. From there it was on to Okinawa, Japan, where I was assigned to a reconnaissance unit operating off of a submarine. Quite a descent: from Big Man on Campus and up-and-coming professional football rookie to a lowly officer hidden in the bowels of a sub. In short, it was just the sort of situation in which a man is finally able to get free of all the distractions and hear what God has to say to him.

And I really needed to hear God's voice. You see, there are few things more miserable than a Christian out of fellowship. I had managed to fool a lot of people in college and in Houston with my "say one thing in public, but live something else in private" lifestyle. But I couldn't fool God. I wasn't even a "good enough" hypocrite to fool myself. I knew I was not in fellowship with Christ. I knew I needed to get my life on track. I knew I had to get back in sync with the Lord.

So in His grace, God pursued me during those early days in the military and stimulated within me an insatiable hunger for the Bible. Who knows why no one told me at the beginning of my Christian life that I needed to get into His Word for myself? But now I was diving into it with extraordinary passion.

As a Marine officer on a submarine, I didn't have any duty. I was just a passenger being taken to my next assignment. So I had nothing but time on my hands. God used that time to give me an in-depth, firsthand exposure to Scripture. And I devoured it! Every spare minute I had I spent reading my Bible. Pouring over it. Looking at various passages again and again. Studying it in my living quarters. Pondering it on my bunk. And later, back at the base, pulling it out to read at the officers' club. Wherever

I went, I'd be off in a corner immersed in God's Word while the other guys were hanging out. I just couldn't get enough of it.

God opened up Scripture as He opened my eyes to see His promises in a way I just accepted and believed them. I'd read a passage and think, "Are you kidding?! He said what?! That's amazing! Oh, Lord, thank You for Your Word!"

I can't really explain it on any other basis than God was revealing Himself to me through His Word. It certainly wasn't anything I was doing. I would just read what the Bible said, and then take it at face value. Accept it. Believe it. And right away my life began to undergo a transformation. This Jesus whom I'd trusted for salvation back in my freshman year of college was now a real Person with whom I was developing a living, thriving, vital relationship.

May I share with you some of the things God showed me as I feasted on His Word?

Chapter 5

DISCOVERING GOD'S PERFECT LOVE

"Grace finds its greatest triumph and glory in the sphere of human weakness." — Francis Schaeffer

One of the first passages of Scripture that made a profound impact on me was 1 John 4:18: "There is no fear in love; but perfect love casts out fear, because fear involves punishment, and the one who fears is not perfected in love."

When I first read that verse, the words "perfect love" jumped out at me. The Bible said God not only loves me, He loves me with *perfect* love. I knew what imperfect love is. I'd seen plenty of that, both in myself and in others. But *perfect* love implies a love that cannot be improved upon. Nothing needs to be added to it. Indeed, nothing can be added to it. It is already complete. It is everything that love can ever be. It is everything that love ought to be. It is, well, *perfect*. This love that God has for me.

Later I read the same verse in *The Living Bible*: "Such love [that is, God's love] has no fear, because perfect love expels all fear. If we are afraid, it is for fear of punishment, and this shows that we have not fully experienced his perfect love."

How does God's "expels all fear" love work? As I reflected on the nature of perfect love, I saw that God does not love in degrees or on different levels. He doesn't love me a little bit, and then a little bit more, and then a little bit more, and so on until He loves me a lot. And it's not as if maybe if I'm good enough, if I measure up enough, if I get close enough to being perfect, why then God will finally love me with the perfect love He is said to have. No! Perfect love means God loves me *perfectly* this very moment. No matter where I am in my maturity with Christ. No matter how long I've been a believer. No matter what my immediate experience may be. God can only love me (and you) in one way—totally, completely, *perfectly*.

How reassuring! In fact, such love gives a solid basis for feeling secure in my relationship with God. You see, if I'm on a performance basis with God, I'm in trouble! Because sooner or later (usually sooner), I'm going to mess up. I'm going to blow it. I'm going to do something that qualifies as sin. If God's love waxes and wanes based on my performance, I will always be afraid He's going to give up on loving me.

Conditional Love

Discovering God's love for me is perfect was unbelievably good news for me, because I had inherited a mind-set that says human beings have to prove themselves to God. In fact, we have to prove ourselves to one another. Such is the case in American culture where I grew up. I had spent my whole life trying to prove myself worthy of other people's love and acceptance. I was driven to establish my value through performance. I was always shooting for the top. Why the top? Because everyone and everything around me made it pretty clear only the people at the top have value: the successful, the beautiful, the intelligent, the rich. Well, I figured I could play that game as well as the next person. So I set out to be the number one quarterback, the most valuable player, the best officer in boot camp, the best Marine in our company, and so on.

I wouldn't have put it this way at the time, but the fact was, I was running scared. I was desperately afraid unless I proved myself "good enough," I would not be loved. I would be rejected.

Years later I discovered the experience of "running scared" is universal. Humans everywhere are terrified that instead of love, they'll get rejection. They fear it from each other. They especially fear it from God. The writer Henri Nouwen described it this way:

> I am so afraid of being disliked, blamed, put aside, passed over, ignored, persecuted, and killed, that I am constantly developing strategies to defend myself and thereby assure myself of the love I think I need and deserve. . . . It takes very little to raise me up or thrust me down. Often I am like a small boat on the ocean, completely at the mercy of its waves. All the time and energy I spend in keeping some kind of balance and preventing myself from being tipped over and drowning shows that my life is mostly a struggle for survival. . . . As long as I keep running about asking: "Do you love me, do you really love me?" I give all power to the voices of the world and put myself in bondage because the world is filled with "ifs." The world says, "Yes, I love you *if* you are good-looking, intelligent, and wealthy. I love you *if* you have a good education, a good job, and good connections. I love you *if*

you produce much, sell much, and buy much." There are endless "ifs" hidden in the world's love. . . The world's love is and always will be conditional.[1]

The world's love is conditional love. It is *if–love*: "I'll love you *if*. . ." What a profound relief, then, to read that God's love is *perfect* love.

The God of perfect love seemed to say: *"John, I love you. Period. No ifs. No conditions. No performance. No degrees of love. I just love you. With infinite, perfect love. I always have. I always will."*

Yes, when we sin and turn away from our heavenly Father, He grieves deeply, and our sin causes us to miss out on His best. But His love for us never goes away. It is eternal, everlasting, ever-perfect.

Does God Love Anyone More Than You?

Wow! That a truly radical thought, and one that can ultimately transform a person's life if he or she begins to accept it, believe it, and experience it. Work with me here as I try to drive home this amazing point with an illustration.

Scripture teaches God is present with us at every moment and in every place. So when you sit down at a Starbucks in the morning to get your shot of caffeine, it may look like you're just sitting there by yourself. But actually there are four persons present: God the Father, God the Son, God the Holy Spirit, and you. Aren't you privileged?

So imagine now you're sitting there sipping your caramel brulée latte *sans* whipped cream, or whatever, and you're just enjoying the Triune God's presence. Bear with me as I employ some sanctified imagination. Suddenly Jesus turns to His Father and says, "Father, I have a question. Whom do You love more—Me or My friend here (meaning you)?" Without a moment's hesitation, the Father looks at Jesus and looks at you and says with a great big smile, "I love you both the same." At that, Jesus claps His hands and exclaims with great joy, "Thank You! That's what I wanted to hear!" Then

Jesus turns to you and asks, "Hey, did you hear that? My Father loves you every bit as much as He loves Me! Isn't that fantastic?!"

I'm not trying to be cute or irreverent. I'm trying to convey a very basic biblical truth that the Father loves you with the same perfect love with which He loves His beloved Son, Jesus. Remember, God does not love in degrees or on different levels. He doesn't love you a lot, but Jesus a whole lot more. He loves you and Jesus both with all the love He has to offer—which is His infinitely perfect love.

When I set the conditional love of the world side by side with God's *perfect love*, it becomes apparent that only God's love is real love. The *if-love* of the world is not love at all. It's bondage. It holds everyone hostage to the fear of rejection.

But suppose you've never heard about God. I encountered countless people in the Soviet Union (and elsewhere around the world) who had never heard about God. I'm not sure you could call them atheists. A true atheist is someone who believes there is no God. Yet, atheism was the official party line of the Soviet regime. But so many of the Soviet people, especially the younger ones who grew up under Communism, have no basis to believe or disbelieve in God because they've never heard about the concept of God to begin with. Imagine their surprise—and for many, their inexpressible joy—to learn there is indeed a God, and He longs to have a personal relationship with them. This truth comes as incredibly good news to them!

Is it still good news for Americans? Or are we pursuing something else when we think about God?

Endnote

[1] Henri J. M. Nouwen, *The Return of the Prodigal Son: A Story of Homecoming* (New York: Doubleday, 1994), 41–42.

Chapter 6

THE PERFORMANCE-
DRIVEN LIFE

"Pursue God, you find happiness.
Pursue happiness, you find neither." — C. S. Lewis

In American culture, most people have heard about God, and most of them have heard that God is a God of love. This sounds good, except that they assume that God's love is just like everyone else's love: it's conditional. It's *if–love*. God will love them *if* they live a good life (whatever that means). *If* they give money to charity. *If* they pay their bills. *If* they don't kill anyone. It's a performance-based system. It's the same approach they take with the rest of their lives: Be the top producer. Come up with all the great ideas. Develop the best body. Become the CEO. Live in the most affluent neighborhood. Get your picture in the social pages. Become the envy of the other mothers. On and on.

There's nothing inherently wrong with being successful, having the best, receiving awards and acclaim, and all the rest of it. After all, God blesses His children in many different ways. The issue is whether we're driven to pursue those things in order to establish our worth, or whether God alone is our supreme desire, and whatever successes He allows us to enjoy we hold with an open hand.

At heart, all human striving is ultimately about love and acceptance. But in a performance-based system, love and acceptance are never guaranteed. They always depend on proving that they are lovable and acceptable. How long can anyone keep that up?

Which is why people who only know about conditional love end up in a self-protective lifestyle, which at its core fosters a life of pretense. They know in their gut they are not nearly as smart, or beautiful, or strong, or powerful, or charming, or whatever it is on the surface makes them appear lovable and acceptable. But they have a vested interest in keeping up "the lie" that they are meeting the conditions of love and acceptance.

In fact, they have no alternative but to keep it up. Because they don't know anything about perfect love. It's off the radar. They don't experience *perfect* love with anyone. Certainly not with other people. And not even with God. *Perfect* love doesn't exist in their world. They are chained to the exhausting demands of conditional love.

Many of the most successful and accomplished people in the world have spoken rather poignantly about the relentless treadmill of performance-based acceptance. Consider, for example, tennis superstar Chris Evert, who dominated women's tennis from the mid–1970s into the 1980s. She won 157 singles championships. And Chris still owns the best win–loss record in singles matches of any professional player in tennis history.

Yet despite her remarkable success, Evert looked back on her tennis career and said, "I had no idea who I was or what I could be away from tennis. I was depressed and afraid because my life had been defined by my being a tennis champion. I was completely lost. Winning made me feel like somebody. It made me feel pretty. It was like being hooked on a drug. I needed the win, the applause, in order to have an identity."[1]

Or take Madonna. One would assume as the world's top-selling female recording artist of all time, having sold more than 300 million records worldwide, and as the most successful solo artist in the history of the Billboard chart, Madonna must live with a great deal of satisfaction. But by her own admission, her life is driven by fear: "My drive in life is from this horrible feeling of being mediocre. And that's always pushing me, pushing me. Because even though I've become somebody, I still have to prove that I'm somebody. My struggle has never ended, and it probably never will."[2]

In a similar way, a man looking back on his life as an extremely successful CEO in the corporate world said, "My life was built on two premises. The first was I could control your opinion and approval of me through my performance. The second was, that was all that mattered in life."

Comments like these sound eerily like those of the character Harold Abrahams in the film *Chariots of Fire*. Several times he describes his tortured motivation to prove himself through running. Whereas Eric Liddell confidently asserted that "[God] made me fast and when I run I feel His pleasure," Abrahams tells his girlfriend that he doesn't love running. "I am more of an addict," he admits. "It's a compulsion with me, a weapon I can use."

Later, as his friend Aubrey rubs him down in preparation for his big Olympic race, he speaks reflectively, "You, Aubrey, are my most complete man. You're brave, compassionate, kind—a content man. That is your secret, contentment. I am 24 and I've never known it. I'm forever in pursuit, and I don't even know what I am chasing. And now in one hour's time I will be out there again. I will raise my eyes and look down that corridor—four feet wide, with ten lonely seconds to justify my whole existence. But *will* I?"[3]

What a miserable existence! To climb all the way to "the top," only to find emptiness there. (For more on futility, read the Old Testament book of Ecclesiastes.)

RADICAL TRUST

Ifs and Oughts

Sadly, a whole lot of Christians are also living in the prison of performance. Yes, they have responded to the gospel message and placed their faith in Christ's death for their sins. Their trust in Christ gives them the hope of eternal life. But from there on, they live as if God decides every day whether He's going to love them or not, depending on what they've done or not done. *If* they go to church. *If* they pray. *If* they read their Bible. *If* they tithe. *If* they don't cuss. *If* they don't use tobacco. *If* they don't cheat on their spouse. If, if, if. . .*then* God will love them.

A lot of this mentality is promoted by much of the teaching Christians hear in their churches. They're told about all of the things they "ought" to do, as if God has given them a checklist of stuff they had better get done, or else He'll be mad. They hear a sermon proclaiming they "ought" to care more about missions. Then they go to a Bible study and hear they "ought" to do good to their neighbor. Then they listen to a preacher on the radio or on a podcast who says they "ought" to work less and spend more time with their families.

It's no wonder as I travel around the country, I hear Christians telling me, "I got some 'oughts' from church this past Sunday. But I haven't even been able to deal with all the I 'oughts' I got the week before."

What a burdensome way to live! In fact, when I hear that sort of thing, I think of the apostle Paul's words: "The letter kills, but the Spirit gives life" (2 Corinthians 3:6, NIV). The "letter" refers to a list of rules, a list of "oughts."

Hearing a long list of "oughts" will never motivate us to live the way our Father longs for us to live. To live like that requires a life-change from the inside out. The Holy Spirit changes us to be more like Jesus. He longs to *ravish* our heart with Christ's perfect love. His grace alone, overflowing with undeserved kindness, is what will motivate us to be obedient to the marching orders of our Lord, who is the true Lover of our souls.

So can we just live any way we want to live, and God will still love us? Well, the short (and perhaps shocking) answer is—yes! The fact that

God's love is a *perfect* love means it will *never* waiver, or be taken away, or be improved upon. No matter what *we* do—whether we are obedient or disobedient to what God asks of us—we cannot increase or decrease His love, because He already loves us with all the love He has. Nothing we do changes His constant love.

But now, let me be clear: When we fail to rest in our Lord's love, the results will be very painful and tragic. It will mean living our lives on earth with our cup half full, going from one temporary fix to another to fill up the other half. The result of that lifestyle will be a colossal waste of our life for Christ's sake and the sake of the gospel.

So yes, we can live any way we want to live, if we choose to. But it means we'll just miss out on experiencing the joy of God's love. However, one outcome we will never see is a change in God's love for us. His *perfect* love will remain steadfast and unchanging. Our sin will make us feel distant from God. But not because He has moved; it's because we have moved. Just as our "good works" cannot increase His love, so our failures cannot decrease it, either.

Make no mistake: Our Father disciplines us. But even that is not done out of anger. Hebrews 12:10 says God disciplines us for our good, which means His correction flows from His love. He *always* seeks our best, and discipline is one way He proves He is our loving Father.

God Is Not Mad at Us

I believe Christians in America desperately need to hear this good news about God's perfect love, because so many of us feel God is mad at us. In our heart of hearts, we feel as if we have failed in our own love for God. And no doubt we have! But we then assume God must be like everyone else—disappointed in us because we have let Him down.

May I say it plainly? **God is not mad!** God has no anger toward us. Do you know why? Because Jesus took all of God's anger upon Himself when He went to the cross. All of our sins, all of our failures, even all of our lukewarm "love" toward God. All of His wrath was placed on Jesus. God cursed Jesus and spent all of His anger on Him, instead of on us:

- "[God] made Him who knew no sin to be sin on our behalf, that we might become the righteousness of God in Him" (2 Corinthians 5:21).
- "But God demonstrates [or proves] His own love toward us, in that while we were yet sinners, Christ died for us" (Romans 5:8).
- "He [that is, God]...did not spare His own Son, but delivered Him over for us all" (Romans 8:32).
- "The life which I now live in the flesh I live by faith in the Son of God, who loved me and gave Himself up for me" (Galatians 2:20).

These verses and many others show us that God's anger is spent. His wrath was poured out on Jesus. God is not mad at human beings. Make no mistake, God hates sin. He hates sin with infinite hatred. With "perfect" hatred, if you will. But He loves sinners with infinite, perfect love.

Rather shocking—and it is! But I believe we need to have our hearts shocked with the awesomeness of God's infinite love. It's the only way we'll ever be "filled up to all the fullness of God," which is what He longs to give us.

And yet there's something even more shocking covered in the next chapter.

Endnotes

[1] Chris Evert, "My Love Match with Andy," *Good Housekeeping* (October 1990): 87-88.

[2] Lynn Hirshberg, "The Misfit," *Vanity Fair* 54 (April 1991): 160-169, 196-202.

[3] *Chariots of Fire*, directed by Hugh Hudson, written by Colin Welland, distributed in North America by Warner Bros., the Ladd Co., and internationally by 20th Century Fox, 1981.

Chapter 7

THE SHOCKING TRUTH
ABOUT JESUS

"God's love for man is the first motive for his acting in grace on behalf of man." — Charles Ryrie

As I pored over Scripture during those early days in the military, I discovered something both amazing and disturbing about Jesus:

> Although He existed in the form of God, [He] did not regard equality with God a thing to be grasped, but emptied Himself, taking the form of a bondservant, and being made in the likeness of men. Being found in

appearance as a man, He humbled Himself by becoming obedient to the point of death, even death on a cross. (Philippians 2:6–8)

This passage teaches that Jesus Christ, who is God, laid aside all of His privileges as God—His glory, His honor, His beauty, His splendor. He "emptied" Himself of all that in order to become like you and me.

I don't know what it's like to be God, but I certainly know what it's like to be a man. And something tells me I were given the choice, I'd choose to be God rather than a man. But Jesus chose to become a man. Without ceasing to be God, He accepted the limitations of a human frame, along with the risks and challenges of living in a fallen world among fallen, sinful people. It would be like the richest man in the world walking away from it all to live at the garbage dump of the worst slum in the world. But Jesus chose to do that for you and me. Second Corinthians 8:9 says, "Do you remember the generosity of Jesus Christ, the Lord of us all? He was rich beyond our telling, yet he became poor for your sakes so that his poverty might make you rich" (PH).

It's almost incomprehensible! In his book *The Reason for God: Belief in an Age of Skepticism,* Tim Keller encourages us to "think of the sun—if you look at its brightness it will blind you. If you move close to it, you'll burn to a crisp. But Jesus is a trillion times more beautiful, glorious, spectacular, and majestic than the sun. Yet He willingly gave up His glory to make you beautiful."

In fact, Jesus went beyond what you and I would do and became our Servant. In John 13, we read about Jesus washing His disciples' feet on the night before His crucifixion. People wore sandals in that culture, and because meals were served at a low table and everyone lay on recliners to eat, no one wanted someone's dirty, smelly feet next to them. So a household slave was assigned the menial task of washing everyone's feet before they came to dinner.

Apparently there was no slave in the Upper Room where Jesus and His disciples were eating. So Jesus took off His robe and assumed the role of a slave and began washing the dirty, smelly feet of His disciples.

Peter objected and basically said, "No way you're going to wash my feet!" Remember, Peter had already recognized Jesus as the Messiah, the Son of God (see Matthew 16:16). He wasn't about to allow the Son of God to suffer the indignity of washing his dirty, smelly feet.

But Jesus replied, "If I do not wash you, you have no part with Me" (John 13:8). Jesus was looking ahead to the way in which His death would wash away Peter's sin. But in doing so, He was also indicating He was playing the role of a Servant for all of us. As He said of Himself, "The Son of Man did not come to be served, but to serve, and to give His life a ransom for many" (Matthew 20:28).

Imagine: God Himself, not only taking on our human form, but taking on the lowliest form a human can take—a slave washing our dirty, smelly feet. God, the most beautiful and glorious Being possible, lays aside all of His beauty and glory for you and for me.

What an awesome thing! But, it's also a disturbing thing, because Jesus allowed even His human form to be marred beyond all recognition. Apparently His appearance was not that impressive to begin with. Isaiah 53:2 tells us that "he had no beauty or majesty to attract us to him, nothing in his appearance that we should desire him" (NIV). Nowadays we make such a big deal of our looks. How would Jesus have fared in our image conscious culture? By all indications, He likely would have been overlooked because apparently He was merely plain, or possibly even ugly, by our standards.

But whatever His actual appearance, Jesus allowed Himself to be beaten so badly the Scripture says "his appearance was so disfigured beyond that of any human being and his form marred beyond human likeness" that people were "appalled" at him (Isaiah 52:14, NIV). If we had been standing there at Calvary and looked at Jesus on the cross, the sight would have made us sick to our stomachs. Quite disturbing—to think that the One who had known infinite beauty in heaven was now reduced to an eyesore.

A Descent into Hell

But the worst of it all was not the physical punishment visited on Jesus. It was the spiritual agony of Jesus taking on the sin of the world—your sin and my sin—and as a result, giving up His connection to His Father as the Father poured out His wrath on sin. The shock of that separation comes screaming out of Jesus' mouth as He cries, "My God, my God, why hast thou forsaken me?" (Matthew 27:46, KJV). I believe this is the only time when Jesus addressed His Father as "God" instead of "Father." Clearly, something happened at the cross that no human mind can ever grasp.

At that moment, when God "made Him who knew no sin to be sin on our behalf" (2 Corinthians 5:21), the eternal union between God the Father and God the Son was in some way broken. Exactly how that separation took place is beyond our understanding as humans. But we know that throughout eternity, the perfect love of the Father for His Son and the perfect love of the Son for His Father had been the nature of their fellowship.

We catch a glimpse of that perfect union and the Father's adoring love of His Son when Jesus was baptized: "After being baptized, Jesus came up immediately from the water; and behold, the heavens were opened, and He saw the Spirit of God descending as a dove and lighting on Him, and behold, a voice out of the heavens said, 'This is My beloved Son, in whom I am well-pleased'" (Matthew 3:16–17).

The same thing happened when Jesus was "transfigured" before Peter, James, and John—that is, His glory was partially revealed to them: "His face shone like the sun, and His garments became as white as light. . .[and] a bright cloud overshadowed them, and behold, a voice out of the cloud said, 'This is My beloved Son, with whom I am well-pleased; listen to Him!'" (Matthew 17:2, 5).

The beloved Son. Through all eternity, Jesus had only known the experience of being God's beloved Son. But on that Friday when He was crucified, the beloved Son became the forsaken Son. And when that happened, Jesus entered hell. Hell is the dwelling place of those who are forsaken by God.

Without doubt, the greatest act of courage in all of time and throughout eternity was Jesus' willing acceptance of the infinite anger and wrath of a Holy God for the sake of our sin. Jesus endured the separation from His Father the way that we should have been separated from Him. It was for my sin and your sin that He was punished, judged, and quite literally went to hell for.

A lot of people today say they don't believe in hell. They can believe in a loving God, but they can't believe in hell. Hell has become politically incorrect. People will say to me, "Maisel, you don't mean to tell me that you believe God is going to send people to hell!" And of course, my response to that is that God doesn't send people to hell—people *choose* hell.

The person who says they don't believe in hell doesn't understand the depth of Christ's love for them. They think they are making God more loving if they say there is no hell. But actually they make Him less loving. You see, there really is a hell. Left to ourselves every one of us would manage to end up there. Yet, God's perfect love cannot allow Him to stand idly by while people die and enter an eternity apart from Him. And so He intervened. Through Christ, God made a way to rescue us from hell.

But consider the cost: Jesus endured an unimaginable separation from God that is the horror of hell. Which tells us something about the depth of Christ's love. Whatever our conception of hell, and whatever the Bible says to describe it, the reality of hell is a trillion times worse than any of us can even imagine. Yet Jesus went to that such an extent to save us from that awful place. How can we not fall on our faces in worship and gratitude and submission to the One who loves us so much? How can we not joyfully and willingly turn our lives over to the One who took our deserved damnation that we might have the free gift of salvation?

I don't know how people who say they don't believe in hell account for the "inconvenient truth" that Jesus totally believed in hell. Indeed, Jesus spoke more about hell than He did about heaven. He did so because He alone understood the eternal consequences awaiting humankind unless a way is provided back to God.

Jesus perfectly understood both the love of God and the wrath of God. Love and wrath were expressed in the same moment, when the Father turned His back on the beloved Son and in infinite, holy anger cursed the sin that His Son had become. In that moment, I again use my sanctified imagination to describe what the Father was saying to you and to me: *Now can you see how much I love you? I will go so far as to turn my back on My beloved Son and let Him suffer the torment of My full wrath and fury and judgment on sin, in order to restore you to the loving relationship I long to have with you.*

In that same moment, I again paraphrase what Jesus was saying to you and to me: *Now can you see how much I love you? I will go so far as to be forsaken by My Father and willingly bear the torment of His full wrath and fury and judgment on sin, in order to restore you to the loving relationship that He longs to have with you.*

What amazing love! Amazing grace. Shocking grace, actually. It is shocking to consider how far Christ would go to restore you and me to the Father.

But did He really have to go that far?

Chapter 8

ARE WE REALLY THAT BAD?

"Some may wish to live within the sound of a church chapel bell. I want to run a rescue shop within a yard of Hell." — C. T. Studd

When I ponder the love of God, I find it both amazing and disturbing. Amazing because of the wonder of His grace toward me. But disturbing, too, because it suggests something awful about me: no matter how sinful or bad or broken I may think I am—and sometimes I think I'm pretty sinful and bad and broken—I'm actually worse! If God had to go all the way to putting Jesus on the cross to save me from my sins, then my sins have to be a whole lot worse than I can ever imagine.

A simple illustration by Dr. Martyn Lloyd-Jones captures the essence of what I'm trying to say. Dr. Jones, a preacher and medical doctor from Wales in the first half of the twentieth century, imagined coming home from a trip and meeting someone who told him, "Oh, while you were gone, a bill came. So I just paid it for you."

Dr. Jones said in the absence of knowing how much his friend had paid, there was no way of knowing how he should respond. If the friend had just paid a little extra postage, that was one thing. But suppose it was hundreds of thousands of pounds (or dollars, in our currency) to pay off a long-standing debt. In that case, Dr. Lloyd-Jones said he would be compelled to fall to his knees and kiss the person's feet in gratitude.

Well, now, Jesus gave up His own life to pay for the debt of my sin. In fact, according to Philippians 2, He gave up His standing in heaven with God the Father. He accepted the limitations of being born a human, and then became a Servant (Slave) to humans. In fact, He allowed the very humans He had created to unjustly condemn Him to death, beat Him to a pulp, and stake Him to two wooden crossbeams in the most horrific form of execution ever devised by man. Then, as He hung on that cross, He actually became my sin and endured God's infinite wrath. All of that to pay my debt. What does that tell you about the size of my debt?

What does that tell you about the size of your debt?

The Worst Sinner in the World

The apostle Paul understood the connection between the size of his sin debt and the enormity of Christ's love for him. In his first letter to his young protégé Timothy, Paul expressed His gratitude to Christ for "appointing me to his service" (1 Timothy 1:12, NIV), that is, allowing Paul to be a spokesperson on behalf of the gospel. I paraphrase what Paul was saying: *Thank You, Lord, for even allowing me to be on Your team.* He felt so honored—and humbled—to be a part of what Christ was doing in the world.

Humility had not always characterized Paul's life. If you read about young Paul (called Saul prior to receiving Christ as Savior) at the end of Acts 7 and the beginning of Acts 8, as well as in the snapshots from his personal narrative in Acts 26, Galatians 1, and Philippians 3, you discover a man who was exceedingly zealous for the Jewish Law, customs, and culture. So much so he violently persecuted those who were turning to Christ as their Messiah. There is a real note of arrogance and self-righteousness in the way Paul decided who was legitimate in God's eyes and who was not.

And that's exactly what Paul tells Timothy about his life before Christ: "I was once a blasphemer and a persecutor and a violent man" (1:13, NIV). How bad was he? Well, to his mind he was so bad that only Christ was able to save him from his sins: "I was shown mercy. . . . The grace of our Lord was poured out on me abundantly. . . . Here is a trustworthy saying that deserves full acceptance: Christ Jesus came into the world to save sinners— *of whom I am the worst.* But for that very reason I was shown mercy so that in *me, the worst of sinners,* Christ Jesus might display his immense patience as an example for those who would believe in him and receive eternal life" (1:13–16, NIV, emphasis added).

Today, when we think of the worst sinners, we point to genocidal dictators and mass murderers and people who commit war crimes and so on. Paul would say his sins topped them all, because he wasn't just sinning against the Christians he put to death, he was sinning against Christ Himself. He spent the first half of his life trying to stamp out Christ. During that time of his life he calls himself a blasphemer: he had insisted Jesus was not God, when in fact Jesus is God.

According to Jewish Law, blasphemy was an unpardonable sin for which one deserved stoning. So in effect, Paul was saying: *I have no business being a part of Christ's church. I of all people should be cursed and stoned, because I blatantly and arrogantly and violently fought Christ. I was not there at His crucifixion, but if I had been, I would not only have been the first to condemn Him, I would have wielded the hammer to drive the nails into His hands. I hated Christ—yes, Christ, who is God Himself! Yet somehow, Christ loved even me, and showed even me His mercy.*

What does the person do who recognizes the enormity of his guilt, yet knows that Christ has paid his debt and forgiven his sins and given him new life? The only appropriate response is the one Paul has in 1 Timothy: He falls to his knees in worship and gratitude and submission, and he praises his Lord, his King, the One who has shown him such immense mercy and grace: "Now to the King eternal, immortal, invisible, the only God, be honor and glory for ever and ever. Amen" (1:17, NIV).

A Debt Forgiven

The remarkable thing is Paul's statement in 1 Timothy is a replay of an incident that had occurred years earlier between Jesus and a self-righteous Pharisee named Simon (see Luke 7:36–50; note Paul had also been a self-righteous Pharisee). The Pharisees were experts in the Hebrew Scriptures and Jewish Law. They exerted considerable authority and influence over the Jewish people.

So one day Simon the Pharisee invited Jesus to come and have dinner with him. Jesus accepted the invitation, and Luke records while the dinner was in progress, a woman who was either a prostitute or a known adulteress showed up, carrying an alabaster vial of perfume. Note an important detail in this account: The fact that the vial was alabaster, coupled with the fact that it held perfume, indicates this woman was holding what amounted to her life's savings.

Recall what I said earlier, in that time people reclined at a low table in order to eat. So Jesus was evidently lying on His side, resting on His arm, with His head toward the table and His feet sticking out at the end of a recliner. The woman came and just stood by His feet. Then she started crying. Not just sniffling, but weeping. Big teardrops fell onto Jesus' feet.

Somehow, guilt and grace had mingled together in this woman's heart. She had perceived the enormity of her sin and her total inability to cover it.

Yet she also recognized Jesus as the only Person who would purchase the redemption and mercy and forgiveness she so desperately needed. She just let her tears do the talking. And then, in gratitude and worship, she kneeled down and wiped away the tears with her hair and began to kiss Jesus' feet. Finally she began pouring out the perfume on His feet as a way of saying: *All that I am and all that I have belongs to You. I am so grateful for Your grace.*

The text says that Simon was shocked that Jesus would allow a known "sinner" to touch Him (along with the fact that contact with a woman was technically forbidden for a rabbi). Jesus, aware of his disdain, asked if He might tell a story.

"Go ahead," Simon replied.

To paraphrase the story from Luke 7: "Once there were two men who owed an investor some money. One of them owed fifty grand, the other guy owed five hundred grand. Unfortunately, both deals went bad, and so both men had to go back to the investor and say, 'You're not going to get your money back.'

"But the investor was a pretty amazing guy. He told each of them, 'Hey, I'm sorry your deal didn't work out. But I'll just absorb the hit. You don't owe me anything.'"

Then Jesus looked at Simon and brought him into the story by asking a question: "Which of these two debtors is going to be more grateful to the investor?"

Simon realized it was a loaded question. So he gave the obvious answer: "I guess the fellow who was in for five hundred grand."

Bingo! Jesus said, in effect, "You got it!" Then He delivered the knock-out punch to the self-righteousness that was on display in that home: "Do you see this woman? I entered your house; you gave Me no water for My feet, but she has wet My feet with her tears and wiped them with her hair. You gave Me no kiss; but she, since the time I came in, has not ceased to kiss My feet. You did not anoint My head with oil, but she anointed My feet with perfume. For this reason I say to you, her sins, which are many, have been forgiven, for she loved much; but he who is forgiven little, loves little."

That woman was like Paul in that she understood the enormity of her sin debt in light of the enormity of Christ's love. Somehow she grasped the "breadth and length and height and depth" of that love, which enabled her to trust Jesus fully and love Him greatly. In truth, her sin debt before God was no greater than Simon the Pharisee's. The difference was she recognized just how sinful she really was and turned to Jesus for mercy.

Simon didn't "get" the point. All he could focus on was the woman's sin. He totally missed the fact that Jesus had come to save that woman from her sin. Worse, he was clueless about the enormity of his own sin. And so, worst of all, he missed the fact that Jesus had come to be his Savior, too.

God Delights in Us

Do you "get" it? Paul's testimony and the story of Simon both lead to the same shocking conclusion: However sinful, bad, or broken you may think you are, *you are actually worse!* But then the truth I hope really shocks your heart—with joy, awe, and gratitude—is this, no matter how much you may think God loves you and has shown grace to you, He *loves you infinitely* more and has poured out infinitely more grace on you than you can even imagine.

Jesus dying on the cross speaks volumes. As He hung on the cross I summarize what Jesus was in effect saying to you and to me: *I value you more than I value Myself. Even though I am being challenged to come down from this cross so as to prove I am the Son of God, I won't do it, because you are precious to Me. I love you more than My own reputation.*

On the cross, I paraphrase Jesus as saying to His Father on my behalf (and on behalf of all of us): *I take all of John's sins—past, present, and future—upon Myself, so that John can have My righteousness, and nothing but pure, perfect love will flow to John from You, Father.*

Because of Jesus' work, the Almighty God will never be mad at me or at you. Yes, Scripture tells us the Father is grieved over our failures and disobedience. But He is sad because we have not trusted Him, and that lack of trust has limited us from following His leading into what is best for us. As a result, we miss out on experiencing His blessing.

By saying *no* to God, we cause Him grief because we have missed out on discovering the "hidden treasure" He has for us, having chosen instead to believe a lie. The Bible calls it the "deceitfulness of sin." Our sin grieves God, but He is no longer angry or mad at us. As indicated earlier, His anger was completely placed on Christ. As a result, we are now the joy of God's heart.

How can that be? When Jesus took your sin and my sin on the cross, He paid off our sin debt and reduced the balance to zero. But He went a step further. Having paid off our sin debt, He then deposited righteousness into our account, so that now we have the righteousness of Jesus. Remember the verse we looked at earlier: "[God] made [Jesus] who knew no sin to be sin on our behalf, *that we might become the righteousness of God in Him*" (emphasis added)?

How righteous do you think Jesus is? Well, when He takes away our sin, He gives us as much righteousness as He has, which means we now have the same standing as Jesus with a holy, righteous God. God no longer views us as sinners but as people who are as righteous as Jesus (thanks to Jesus).

So just as Jesus is God's beloved Son, now those of us who are in Christ are also God's beloved sons and daughters. The Father delights in us just as much as He delights in Jesus. And in fact, that is exactly what Jesus asked His Father to do as He was preparing to go to the cross: "I have made you known to them, and will continue to make you known in order that *the love you have for me may be in them* and that I myself may be in them," (John 17:26, NIV, emphasis added).

I like the way *The Living Bible* phrases this verse: "You love them as much as you love me."

Chapter 9

WHAT IS LOVE?

"Love is from God. . .for God is love." —1 John 4:7–9

What God thinks and feels about each member of His family were profound thoughts boiling in my mind as a young Marine officer riding around in a submarine (and those thoughts have continued to percolate in my mind and heart ever since). They had the feel of things that are too good to be true. Yet I knew because God had said them, they had to be true. In fact, if God said them, they were too good not to be true.

But there was one core understanding that really tied all of this together for me and formed an unassailable bedrock of confidence in God's love. It has to do with what we mean by "the love of God." I've been using that phrase again and again. What exactly does it mean? How do we define God's "love"?

The word *love* is used in so many ways nowadays it's become a meaningless term. I hear guys say they "love" golf, or they "love" hunting, or they "love" this or that sports team. People say they "love" chocolate, or they "love" going to the movies, or they "love" their car. A guy will say, "Oh, I love my wife," but then I watch the way he treats her and I think, "Really?" And of course a lot of our culture uses the term "love" when it really means "lust."

Recall the I♥NY campaign ("I Love New York"), with the heart symbol substituting for the word "love"? Now you see signs parodying that campaign by spelling out the symbol: "I Heart This or That."

So how does any of that help us understand the idea that God "loves" us?

It doesn't, which is why we have to go to the Bible itself to appreciate the meaning of "love" when that term is used in relation to God. In the New Testament, the Greek root word *agape* is translated "love" and is used most often to describe God's love. For instance:

- God so loved (*agape*) the world that He gave His only begotten Son (John 3:16).
- You shall love (*agape*) the Lord your God with all your heart, and with all your soul, and with all your mind. . . . You shall love (*agape*) your neighbor as yourself (Matthew 22:37–39).
- Love (*agape*) is patient, love (*agape*) is kind. . . . But now faith, hope, love (*agape*), abide these three; but the greatest of these is love (*agape*) (1 Corinthians 13:4–8, 13).
- God is love (*agape*) (1 John 4:6).
- In this is love (agape), not that we loved (*agape*) God, but that He loved (*agape*) us (1 John 4:10).

So what does *agape* mean? In his profoundly insightful book, *The Four Loves,* C. S. Lewis describes *agape* as the highest form of love in that it is selfless. It involves a passionate commitment to another person's well-being with no expectation of getting "paid back." This description certainly describes God's perfect love for us.

Another person who deeply affected my understanding of God's agape kind of love was the late Dr. Harold Hoehner, a professor of systematic theology at Dallas Theological Seminary. His excellent work on the book of Ephesians helped me see that *God shows His love in that He always seeks that which is best—meaning the highest good—for the object of His love.* So when Scripture says that God "loves" us, it means that every motivation our Father has toward us is found in His desire and commitment to seek that which is our highest good.

Loving Like a Parent

Of course, definitions can sound rather dry. What really brings that definition of love home to me—quite literally—is it describes my feelings as a parent for my daughter A'Dina. As she was growing up, I just instinctively felt an intense desire to seek what I believed to be her highest good. I'm not saying I was perfect in doing that, or that I always knew what was actually best for her. But imperfect as I was, I sincerely wanted the best for my child. I think most parents do.

I mean, suppose your child had a life-threatening condition. Wouldn't you as a parent do just about anything to remedy the situation? If their kidney was failing and they needed a new one, wouldn't you say, "Here, take one of mine"? If they needed a blood transfusion, wouldn't you say, "Here, take some of my blood"? Indeed, I've stood at the side of more than a few parents whose son or daughter was going through some terrible ordeal, and I've heard them say, "I would trade places with my child in a heartbeat if I could." What drives that sentiment? Love!

And in fact, Jesus encouraged us to use our family relationships as a way to perceive God's deep, abiding, passionate, almost irrational commitment of love toward us. "Which of you," Jesus observed, "if your son asks for bread, will give him a stone? Or if he asks for a fish, will give him a snake?" (Matthew 7:9–10, NIV).

The obvious answer to both of those hypothetical scenarios is that no loving parent would do such a thing! Not in Jesus' day, not in our day. Indeed, parents today go to great lengths to try and make their children whole and happy. They actively seek out the best schools, the best coaches, the best doctors, the best cars, the best colleges, the best of everything for their children.

A loving parent even endures the wails of her child as she packs him into the car for a visit to the dentist. "Mommy, I don't want to go to the dentist!" Mommy knows that full well. She knows that filling the boy's cavities is going to hurt him. But she takes him to the dentist anyway, because she wants what is best for her son. Unconditional love motivates us to seek what is best for the other person.

Jesus picked up on that instinctive parental concern for one's children and continued, "If you, then, though you are evil, know how to give good gifts to your children, how much more will your Father in heaven give good gifts to those who ask him!" (Matthew 7:11, NIV).

Jesus is saying, even though human parents instinctively love their children deeply and sincerely, their love remains inherently imperfect, since all human parents are sinners. Yet even sinful parents, who can only express imperfect love, still love their imperfect children by trying to do what is best for them. Well, multiply that devoted, even if imperfect, love by a trillion, and you will begin to catch a glimpse of God's unchanging, everlasting, incorruptible, perfect love for His imperfect children—you and me. God's love requires Him to *always* seek what is our highest good, not just once in a while!

Love Involves Risk

"Okay, John, that sounds great," you may be saying. "I love hearing these wonderful things, and I want them to be true. I really do. But what about the Ethiopian guy you talked about at the beginning. He ended up in prison for telling people about Jesus, and most likely got killed for it. How can you say that outcome was for his 'highest good'?"

Well, now you can see where the second part of this book comes into play. It's one thing to celebrate God's perfect love and to ponder it in all its glory. But at some point we have to start trusting His love and acting on it—making conscious decisions that depend on God's love being as real and true and perfect as the Bible tells us it is.

In other words, we have to take a risk. Love always involves risk. Indeed, love *invites* us to risk. Remember our premise?

Our willingness to surrender to God is directly related to the depth of our belief that God really loves us with perfect love.

So the more we trust God's love, the more risk we'll be willing to take in surrendering to what He asks of us.

Love always involves risk. Love always invites risks. A young man can tell his girlfriend a hundred thousand times he loves her, and of course she will love hearing these meaningful words. But then comes the day when he builds up his courage to take her to some romantic spot, fall on his knee, pull out a diamond ring, look into her eyes, and ask, "Will you marry me?" He's taking a risk, because she might reject his request.

For her part, the young lady is now presented with a risk of her own. Can she trust that young man's love? Can she trust what he has declared a hundred thousand times—that he will be there for her, protect her, provide for her, adore her, delight in her, and devote himself to her? The young man awaits her response. And of course he is hoping, more than anything else, that she will trust his love and declare, "Yes!"

In a rather similar way, God has declared countless times to you and to me, both in His Word and through His Son, Jesus: *I love you.* Of course we love hearing these words. We're like, "That's great! How wonderful!" But inevitably the time comes—and it comes daily—when God says, *Trust Me!* He is taking a risk, because we might, and often do, say, "No."

But His invitation also presents us with a risk. Will we trust God's love? Will we trust what He has declared a hundred thousand times—that He will be there for us, protect us, provide for us, adore us, delight in us, and devote Himself to us? What we do next says everything that needs to be said as to whether we really believe God when He says: *I love you.*

"TRUST ME!"

PART II

priceless. But all of that happe
learn the art of war and th
So you can see I was bei
the next chapter in m
whether I'd learne
If ever th
goodness,
war fou
was

GOD STOPS ME
IN MY TRACKS

"He knows the way He takes, even if for the moment we do not."
— J. I. Packer

For me, the risk of trusting God's love and acting on it came courtesy of the United States Marine Corps. After a year in Okinawa, the Marines sent me home for a year. Then one day I received my orders to report for assignment in Vietnam.

Of course, I knew that day would come. After all, Uncle Sam had not sent me to Okinawa to enjoy a personal spiritual retreat! Yes, it worked out that I got to do a lot of in-depth study of Scripture while I was there. This encounter with God and His Word proved life-changing. It was utterly

ned in my spare time. My real job was to

science of commanding soldiers in combat.

g prepared both spiritually and professionally for

life. When the orders came down, it was time to see

anything in either regard.

re was a setting devised to test one's belief in God's love and

ietnam was that setting. Not the place or the people, but the

ght there. The place and the people were beautiful. But the war I

ent into was nothing short of a living hell.

As soon as I had my assignment and my unit, we were sent out on an operation into a "hot zone," meaning an area where we were highly likely to encounter the enemy. As a young lieutenant, I was feeling that same intense pressure I'd always felt to prove myself. I wanted to perform well and professionally in my new assignment, especially since lives were involved.

Unfortunately, the realities of combat in Vietnam had little regard for the ambitions of a young lieutenant. The enemy's strategy involved guerrilla warfare, and as soon as we came under fire, everything started going haywire.

Right in the middle of all the mayhem, some South Vietnamese soldiers with whom we were working brought in a Vietcong they had captured and set him in front of me. I had all the adrenalin of the battle racing around in my system, so in anger I seized the prisoner and threw him down on the ground just as hard as I could, as if he was the sole cause of the war.

Right then, the Spirit of God stopped me cold and spoke directly to my spirit with a shouting conviction that was crystal clear: "If your enemy is hungry, feed him; if he is thirsty, give him something to drink" (Romans 12:20, NIV, quoting Proverbs 25:21).

It was a passage I had read with keen interest during my time in Okinawa. Here's the larger context:

> Never pay back evil for evil to anyone. Respect what is
> right in the sight of all men. If possible, so far as it depends

on you, be at peace with all men. Never take your own revenge, beloved, but leave room for the wrath of God, for it is written, "Vengeance is mine, I will repay," says the Lord. "But if your enemy is hungry, feed him, and if he is thirsty, give him a drink; for in so doing you will heap burning coals on his head." Do not be overcome by evil, but overcome evil with good. (Romans 12:17–21)

Needless to say, I had a real conflict on my hands! I was looking at a man who, moments before, had been intent on killing me and as many of my men as possible. Now his fate was up to me. Yet here was God telling me to treat him with compassion. What was I going to do?

I have learned since that the Holy Spirit often intervenes in a believer's life at key moments to direct their actions. Often He brings a passage of Scripture to mind, as He did on that occasion. At other times He may just introduce a thought or otherwise make it plain what He wants us to do: "John, strike up a conversation with that man." "John, call this person." "John, cancel that trip." Theologians call this the "leading" of the Spirit.

Whatever it's called, the point is anything and everything God tells us to do is always sourced in His perfect love for us. God has, in effect, locked Himself into a law that I would summarize as: *I cannot do anything with My power, plan, or purpose for you or to you that does not involve your highest good. So if I ask you to do a certain thing, it's because I intend your highest good.*

A Defining Moment

Now this is where the issue of trust gets very gritty. Because sometimes God asks us to do something that looks very risky or feels very scary. It certainly doesn't look like our highest good. So we look at it and say, "Really, Lord? You really want me to do what? Are You sure?" At other times, He asks us to do something that totally goes against what we feel like doing. And sometimes it goes against what everyone around us thinks we ought to do.

This encapsulates the dilemma I was facing as I stood over that prisoner. Was I going to follow the Spirit's prompting, or not?

"If your enemy is hungry, feed him, and if he is thirsty, give him a drink."

The Lord's voice had stopped me in my tracks. Everyone around me was yelling in a frenzy. But I was strangely quiet. The world kind of shifted into slow motion. I looked down at the captive, cowering on the ground where I'd thrown him, visibly shaking with fear as to what was going to happen next. My eyes fastened on his lips, which were visibly parched. So, moved by the terribly convicting words of the Spirit, I reached for my canteen and knelt down to help the prisoner to his feet.

At that moment, the South Vietnamese began shouting, "No, no, no!" But I pushed them away as I lifted him up, and then I handed him my canteen. He took it, trembling all over, and began to drink.

That's when the Lord spoke to me a second time: "John, people are precious. *All* people are precious to Me."

Those words were like a battering ram colliding with my perspective on the Vietcong. I sensed the Spirit was seeking to break through to me and get me to see I could no longer view my enemy the way I'd been viewing them. He was asking me to see the Vietcong as people—people who were precious in the eyes of Jesus.

Yes, the same Jesus who told His followers, "You have heard that it was said, 'You shall love your neighbor and hate your enemy.' But I say to you, love your enemies and pray for those who persecute you, so that you may be sons of your Father who is in heaven" (Matthew 5:43–45). Jesus loved His enemies. The Spirit was confronting me with the reality that if I was going to follow Jesus, I would have to allow some of my thinking to be changed.

That incident became a defining moment in my life. After it was over, I honestly can't recall having any feelings of hatred left for the Vietcong.

Yes, they were the enemy, and my responsibility was to protect my men, and we were at war. But what happened that day definitely caused me to start thinking about them in a different light.

Later I saw a chopper full of V-C (Vietcong) who had been killed. I remember staring at them and feeling profoundly sad. I realized they had passed into a Christ-less eternity because no one had told them about the Redeemer. This awareness made me deeply sorrowful about the war.

Following Orders—But Whose?

Without question, trying to see the Vietcong as precious in God's sight put me in some pretty awkward situations at times. For example, several weeks after the incident with the prisoner, I was out on patrol with my team again when we came across several Vietcong who were badly wounded. We were the rear guard on the operation, and the point patrol ahead of us had shot the V-C and left them for dead. When we realized they were still alive, I called my commanding officer and explained what was happening. He said, "Waste 'em," meaning to finish them off.

Given what the Spirit had started me thinking about, I was now faced with a dilemma. Only days earlier, He had impressed upon me very clearly that *all* people matter to God—even wounded Vietcong. In that previous situation, I had acted out of blindness and fury until the Lord rebuked me with His Word. This time, however, I had no excuse. The words "people are precious" were still ringing in my ears.

On the other hand, my CO (commanding officer) had indicated his decision in no uncertain terms. What was I supposed to do—disobey him and risk getting court-martialed?

I don't want any misunderstanding here. I had not suddenly turned into some super-spiritual model of piety on the battlefield. Nor did I feel in any way morally superior to my CO or anyone else in the war. I certainly didn't have all the answers to the ethical and moral challenges we were facing on a regular basis. I was just a young officer trying to come to grips with what Jesus had told me about people. Now I was in a situation that was testing me, testing whether my "trust" in God was for real or merely superficial.

I in no way wanted to countermand my CO's directive. But I had already made up my mind that if God said all people are precious in His sight, then I could not—would not—treat my enemies cruelly. So, by God's grace and strength, and after being encouraged that several of my guys were willing to carry the wounded men out of the jungle with me, I got back on the line to my CO and said, "Sir, I'm going to bring them out."

I know he didn't like hearing that, but he didn't stop me, either. In fairness to him, I should point out we had to carry the Vietcong a long way on a path that cut us off from the main body of the company. This isolation increased our exposure to enemy attack, and we were in a hot area. So I'm sure my CO was largely motivated by concern for our safety and didn't want us to risk our lives over a few badly wounded enemy. In the end, we managed to bring the wounded men out and put them on a chopper back to an aid station.

Chapter 11

TRUST IS TIED
TO GOD'S SOVEREIGNTY

"I am waiting on Thee, Lord, to open the way." — Hudson Taylor

I never found out what happened to those wounded Vietcong soldiers. But then, a lot of things happen in our lives where we aren't told the final outcome. Which brings me to a crucial point in terms of fighting the battle for faithfulness to God: the only way a person can trust that God is committed to their highest good, and act on that trust, is if they accept that God is in control over everything that happens with perfect knowledge of everything that happens. In other words, God is sovereign and He is omniscient. In *everything*.

RADICAL TRUST

Martin Luther summed it up about as well as anyone can:

> When [God] makes promises, you ought to be out of
> doubt that He knows, and can and will perform, what He
> promises; otherwise, you will be accounting Him neither
> true nor faithful, which is unbelief, and the height of
> irreverence, and a denial of the most high God! And
> how can you be thus sure and certain, unless you know
> that certainly, infallibly, immutably and necessarily, He
> knows, wills, and will perform what He promises? Not
> only should we be sure that God wills, and will execute
> His will, necessarily and immutably; we should glory in
> the fact, as Paul does in Romans 3: "Let God be true, and
> every man a liar" (verse 4), and again, "Not that the word
> of God has failed" (Romans 9:6), and in another place,
> "The foundations of God standeth sure, having this seal,
> the Lord knoweth them that are His" (2 Timothy 2:19).
> In Titus 1, he says: "Which God, that cannot lie, prom-
> ised before the world began" (verse 2). And Hebrews
> 11:6 says: "And without faith it is impossible to please
> God, because anyone who comes to him must believe
> the he exists and that he rewards those who earnestly
> seek him."[1]

Confident certainty about God's sovereignty is where a lot of
people get stuck. They don't accept that God is in control over everything. They love the idea of God loving them and having their highest
good in view. But then something comes along that doesn't appear to be
for their highest good, like a life-threatening illness, or the tragic death
of their child, or the loss of their job, or some other calamity. At that
point, their "trust" in God starts to waiver because their situations appear
to be an exception to God's sovereignty.

The word "appears" is the key. A. W. Tozer, a pastor and author in the first half of the twentieth century, pointed out that "to the child of God, there is no such thing as an accident. He travels an appointed way. . . . Accidents may indeed *appear* to befall him and misfortune stalks his way; but these evils will be seen *in appearance only* and will *seem* evil only because we cannot read the secret script of God's hidden providence."[2] Clearly, what God sees and knows is very different from what we humans see or know. For this reason Paul urges us to walk by faith, not by sight (see 2 Corinthians 5:7).

The story of Joseph in the Old Testament illustrates what it means to walk by faith, not by sight. His brothers sold him into slavery. Next, he was traded to the Egyptians and made a household servant. Then, his master's wife framed him and he was thrown into prison. Later, he befriended one of the inmates there, who happened to have standing with the Pharaoh and promised to put in a good word for Joseph when he got out. But instead that "friend" totally forgot, so Joseph remained in prison another two years. At that point, he interpreted one of Pharaoh's dreams, and as a result he was appointed second-in-command over Egypt. Indeed, he experienced a reversal of fortune, for sure, but it still didn't change the fact that Joseph would spend much of his life separated from his family, and that all of his adult life would be lived in a foreign land.

Then one day Joseph's brothers showed up—the same brothers who had betrayed him in the first place. Had he chosen to, he could have exacted sweet revenge upon them. He had full power to do so. And once he revealed who he was to them, they assumed he would use that power to "waste 'em." But instead Joseph said, "Do not be afraid, for am I in God's place? As for you, you meant evil against me, but God meant it for good in order to bring about this present result, to preserve many people alive" (Genesis 50:19–20).

God meant it for good. This is what it means to walk by faith! This perspective comes from holding onto the truth that God is sovereign *no matter what.* No matter the tragedy. No matter the trial. No matter the trouble. No matter the tears. "God causes all things to work together for good to those who love God, to those who are called according to His purpose" (Romans 8:28). *All* things!

For Joseph, "all things" included: the betrayal of his brothers; the shame and humiliation of being a slave; the injustice of being imprisoned for a crime he did not commit; the racial prejudice that probably played a big part in why his master took his wife's word over Joseph's; the dashing of his hopes for an early release from prison; the years of not knowing what had happened to his family, and especially his father; the emotional pain he clearly lived with throughout his life, which bubbled to the surface when his brothers arrived.

Given those circumstances, we can easily imagine Joseph saying what a lot of us say to God when He asks us to walk a difficult journey: "Really, Lord? You really want me to go through all of this? Are You sure?" But Joseph recognized God is in control, *no matter what.* He had a radical commitment to the truth that God, in His love, would use *everything* that touched Joseph to accomplish His will for Joseph. Not everything that happened to Joseph was good. But God would use even the evil Joseph experienced for Joseph's highest good, as well as for God's greater purposes.

God Never Wastes Our Sorrows

The point is, God never wastes His children's sorrows. No matter what hurt or pain or disappointment or shattered dreams we've experienced, we must cling to the fact that God has a good purpose for *every* sorrow.

As the theologian R. C. Sproul puts it in his book *The Invisible Hand*, "For the Christian every tragedy is ultimately a blessing, or God is a liar."

Of course, tragedies and sorrows don't feel good or look good. But that's not what matters. What matters is God has locked Himself into a law that says He will accomplish His highest good for us even out of our sorrows—in His time, and in His way. As the early church father Augustine is quoted as saying, "God judged it better to bring good out of evil than to suffer no evil to exist" (St. Augustine, Enchiridion, xxvii). So our sorrows *will* turn out to have a purpose behind them. They are not random. Good will come of them. In God's time, and in God's way.

And we can add: *with God's Son.* In Romans 8, right after declaring that "God causes all things to work together for good," Paul follows up on that thought with the rhetorical question: "He who did not spare His own Son, but delivered Him up for us all, how will He not also *with Him* freely give us all things?" (v. 32, emphasis added). Our highest good will always come to us through and with Jesus. You see, if something we get doesn't involve Jesus, then it's not our highest good. In fact, it's not good at all.

Indeed, the ultimate proof that God uses *everything* to accomplish His good purposes is Jesus' own death on the cross. The cross was the greatest evil ever committed. Yet through the cross God brought about the greatest good any of us can ever know: forgiveness of our sins and a restored relationship with God.

What enabled Jesus to face the cross? It was not merely human courage. The account of Jesus' agony in the garden of Gethsemane (see Matthew 26:37–44) shows even He flinched as He contemplated the realities of what was coming. I paraphrase His prayer: *Father, isn't there another way? Can't I drink a different cup? I've read Psalm 22 (which prophetically describes the agony the Messiah would face), and it doesn't look good. I would really like You to consider whether there might not be a Plan B on this matter of a crucifixion.* But then His prayer changed tone: *You know what, Father? I want You to know I'm all in with the way You've arranged things, if that's the best way to bring about Your glory. Not My will, but Yours be done!*

Why could Jesus say that? Because He knew His Father loved Him perfectly. He knew that the Father would never ask Him to go through the shame and agony of the cross and the horror of breaking their fellowship unless the Father's love had His highest good in view. So He could say (again, I paraphrase), *I'm willing to trust. If You say drink the cup, I'm going to drink the cup.*

Jesus also knew His Father was sovereign, and nothing that touched Him was outside of the Father's control. You can see trust in action immediately following the scene in the garden. Jesus wakes up His disciples and they prepare to leave, but just then Judas appears with a mob to arrest Jesus. The disciples are confused and afraid. Peter, ever impetuous, whips out a sword and prepares to do battle. Clearly, he was looking at the situation from the human perspective.

We can imagine the other disciples were doing the same. Perhaps some of them might have been thinking, *Well, isn't this just great—betrayed by one of our own guys! We should have never let Judas become one of us. Who vetted him, anyway? Who did his screening interview?*

Someone else may have been thinking, *Wow, we've managed to walk right into a trap! Whose brilliant idea was that? James, you're the guy who always seems to plan out where we're going. Why'd you have to pick this route? Now we're done for!*

By contrast, Jesus doesn't do any of that. He sees what is happening and simply receives it from the Father's hand: "Shall I not drink the cup that the Father has given me?" (John 18:11, NIV). He is totally at peace because He trusts that His Father is in total control.

Soon afterward, Jesus stands before Pilate, who tells Him, "Do You not know that I have authority to release You, and I have authority to crucify you?"

Again, Jesus affirms His Father's sovereignty by replying, "You would have no authority over Me, unless it had been given you from above" (John 19:10–11).

God Is the Only Circumstance

Either God is in control over everything, or else He is not in control over anything. Or, as someone else has put it, "Christ is either Lord of all, or He is not Lord at all."

Likewise, Jerry Bridges, author of *Trusting God: Even When Life Hurts* and other book titles, who has been a longtime member of the Navigators, notes that "if there is a single event in the entire universe that can occur outside of God's sovereign control, then we cannot trust Him. His love may be infinite, but His power is limited and His purposes can be thwarted."[3] In other words, we wouldn't have a sovereign Lord.

But we do! God is sovereign and He is committed to our highest good. Therefore, nothing will touch us except what He allows. And whatever He allows He will cause to work together for our highest good.

Which means we no longer allow our circumstances to determine our reality. "The only circumstance in life is God," Hudson Taylor, founder of the China Inland Mission, is reputed to have said. In other words, the determinative reality in the universe is the truth that God is committed to us with a love that is all-perfect and all-powerful. This bedrock truth must grip us when various circumstances compete for our attention and tempt us to end up in fear.

It is fear that drives countless people—even Christians. The fear of going broke and not having enough. The fear of rejection and not getting the job or the promotion. The fear of failure and not getting the sale or winning the contract or funding the project. The fear of abandonment and losing the relationship. Ultimately the fear of death and not being ready for what one will face on the other side.

Fears like these are real, in the sense human beings inevitably will experience them. Yet they are not based in reality, if indeed "the only circumstance in life is God." Our all-loving, all-powerful Father will bring about our highest good even if He asks us to face bankruptcy or poverty, rejection or scorn, failure or disappointment, abandonment or loneliness—even death and dying. *God will never waste our sorrows.*

For that reason, rather than giving in to fear, God invites us to give in to faith, which expresses itself in gratitude for everything that comes our way: "Give thanks in all circumstances, for this is God's will for you in Christ Jesus" (1 Thessalonians 5:18, NIV). And Colossians 3:15 instructs us to dedicate ourselves to being thankful.

A thankful heart *in every circumstance* is a heart that is responding to the grace and love of God. "The Lord longs to be gracious to you,"

RADICAL TRUST

Isaiah reminds us. "He waits on high to have compassion on you." What an incredible thought, that God *longs* to pour out His grace on each of us at each moment of our existence, so that we experience more and more of His marvelous lovingkindness. If we'll trust that lovingkindness and embrace what God sends our way with gratitude, we'll experience the blessing God intends for us: "How blessed are all those who long for Him" (Isaiah 30:18).

So how did faith and gratitude work on the battlefield in Vietnam?

Endnotes

1 Adapted from John Dillenberger, ed., *Martin Luther: Selections from His Writings* (New York: Anchor Books, 1962).

2 A. W. Tozer, *We Travel an Appointed Way* (Camp Hill, PA: Wingspread Publishers, 2010), 3-4.

3 Jerry Bridges, *Trusting God: Even When Life Hurts* (Colorado Springs: NavPress, 1989), 37.

Chapter 12

CRAZY TRUST

"Worry is putting questions marks where God has put periods."
— John R. Rice

By God's grace, during my early days in Vietnam, I set my mind on pursuing a radical commitment to the love of God and the sovereignty of God. Everything I'd read in the Bible seemed to emphasize God's control over *everything* that takes place on a battlefield.

For example, to the Israelites who were getting ready to cross the Jordan River and launch a military campaign to capture Canaan, Moses said, "Be strong and courageous, do not be afraid or tremble at them [the

Canaanites], for the LORD your God is the one who goes with you. He will not fail you or forsake you" (Deuteronomy 31:6).

Likewise, David, who was a warrior if ever there was one, went into battle with total confidence in God:

> The Lord is my light and my salvation;
> Whom shall I fear?
> The Lord is the defense of my life;
> Whom shall I dread? . . .
> Though a host encamp against me,
> My heart will not fear;
> Though war arise against me,
> In spite of this I shall be confident. (Psalm 27:1, 3)

Based on passages like these, I gave in to a belief that God would be my shield, my refuge, and my fortress—*no matter what*. This confidence in Him led to a deeply held conviction that no bullet would touch me unless God allowed it. And if He allowed it, then He had a purpose for it, and that purpose would be for my highest good.

Likewise, if I lost a leg or an arm, it would only be because God wanted to accomplish something greater through me without that limb than He could have if I was all in one piece.

As the preacher Charles Spurgeon has been quoted (I learned later), "If any other condition had been better for you than the one in which you find yourself, divine love would have placed you there."[1]

And what if I caught a bullet between the eyes? Well, no big deal. Psalm 31:15 said my times were in His hands anyway. So if he chose to end my life in combat, that was okay by me, because in the next moment I would be standing before Jesus!

Again, either God is in control over everything, or else He is not in control over anything. His sovereignty includes being in control of when we die. It seemed to me because of God's sovereignty, every believer is immortal until God is through with them. That truth basically snuffed out the fear of dying for me.

Again, the confidence of David became my confidence:

You know when I sit down and when I rise up. . . .
You scrutinize my path and my lying down,
And are intimately acquainted with all my ways. . . .
Where can I go from Your Spirit?
Or where can I flee from Your presence? . . .
If I make my bed in Sheol [the place of the dead],
    behold, You are there. . . .
If I say, "Surely the darkness will overwhelm me,
And the light around me will be night,"
Even the darkness is not dark to You,
And the night is as bright as the day,
Darkness and light are alike to You.
(Psalm 139:2, 3, 7, 8, 11–12)

To know my heavenly Father was watching over *everything* that touched me, and to know that He was beside me in *every* circumstance totally freed me up to revel in my relationship with Jesus—even as war was raging all around me. Jesus became so real to me! I might be sitting in the mud in a foxhole, with rain pouring down, but I would be talking to Jesus, just laughing and having the greatest time with Him, and worshiping Him. Or I might be in the middle of a firefight, running through the jungle, with guys yelling and guns firing and bullets zipping all over the place. But again, I would be laughing and calling out to Jesus, with a profound sense of His presence right there beside me. I mean, it was real!

As I look back on it, I can see that my willingness to surrender to whatever God might allow to happen to me flowed directly out of a confidence that He really loved me with a perfect love. It was not a confidence that I was trying to find in my own strength. It was just a natural response to a growing realization that God was passionately committed to my highest good, and that He had the power to bless and protect me.

It seemed like everywhere I turned, God was shouting His promise to me: "John, I love you! Trust Me!" So how could I not trust Him? Sometimes when we would be assaulting a position, I would even laugh and say, "Okay, Lord, is this going to be it? Are you about to take me out of here? If so, I'm ready. If not, that's okay, too." This mind-set vividly illustrates how personal and intimate the sense of Christ's presence became to me.

You see, I really believe we Christians are immortal until God is through with us on earth. We don't have to fear death because we can't die until God is ready to take us home. This God-confidence leads to a message Christians in the West desperately need to hear today: *Don't play it safe!*

I believe R. C. Sproul nailed it when in essence he said, "The greatest need in the church today is passion to discover the true identity of God. It would revolutionize Christians' lives; it would revolutionize the church."[2] Unfortunately, the world has intimidated us to live like cowards. Because of my experience of Christ's presence, one of the biggest benefits of not having to play it safe in the firefights of Vietnam was I began to be less concerned about myself and more concerned for the others around me.

Endnotes

[1] Quoted by Jim Reiman, *Evening by Evening: The Devotions of Charles Spurgeon* (Grand Rapids, MI: Zondervan, 2010).

[2] Based on an interview given at www.centralpc.org/sermons/2000/s000409.htm, accessed on Nov. 18, 2011.

Chapter 13

LEARNING TO OBEY– THE HARD WAY

"To go as I am led, to go when I am led, to go where I am led."
— A. T. Pierson

My security in God's sovereignty freed me to start looking out for my men rather than myself. I reasoned that if God was in control of everything, then there was no room for me to play it safe. The game was no longer about getting myself out of Vietnam alive; it was about getting my men ready for eternity by introducing them to Jesus. I knew I could die, but my men couldn't die, because they weren't ready to go into eternity.

RADICAL TRUST

Unfortunately, God had to use a terrible experience to open my eyes to this reality. We were on a difficult patrol, and I made a bad decision out of my own selfishness and disobedience to God. I was still learning that obeying God is not just saying, "Yes, Lord," when God tells us to do something. It's saying, "Yes, Lord—*no matter what!*"

My unit had been on the trail for several days. We were utterly exhausted. When night came, we set a watch and I fell into a deep sleep between two boulders. After just a few hours, my men came and woke me up. But I couldn't open my eyes. In that brief period of sleep, my eyes had matted shut. I was spent! The guys literally had to get a canteen of water and pull my eyelids apart.

We slugged through the next day, and then in the evening we camped in the jungle. When darkness fell, it turned out to be a breathtaking night. I don't think even a Colorado night sky could compare to what it looks like in the pitch darkness of the jungle. I was seeing countless stars, and they were dancing. It was unbelievable!

About that time, a fellow lieutenant named Carl remarked to me in the darkness, "Wow, John! Isn't that magnificent?"

I replied, "It sure is! You know, that's what God created."

Carl answered back, "Yeah, you couldn't look at that and not know that there's a God."

I seized upon his statement and said, "There really is a God, Carl, and that God calls each one of those stars by name."

He said, "Really?"

I said, "Yeah. And did you know that the God who designed these heavens wants to have a relationship with you. He wants to know you in a personal way?"

Carl paused a second, and then he said enthusiastically, "Man, I would love to know about that!"

Then, I made my terrible decision. It was late. I was even more tired than I'd been the night before. I knew we would be getting under way at first light. We had another hard day's trek ahead of us. So I said,

"I'll tell you what. It's getting kind of late. When we get back to base camp in the next couple of days, let's you and me get together. I'd like to explain to you what the Bible says about how you can have that relationship with God."

Carl said, "Man, I will look forward to that, John!"

"Great," I replied, and we shoved off. Before long I was sound asleep.

The next day Carl caught a bullet through the throat and died. When I learned about his death, I was profoundly shaken. I realized that a man had told me he was thirsty for Jesus, the Living Water of life, and I hadn't given him that water. I'd told him I'd do it later. I was tired and thinking more about my own desire for physical rest than Carl's desire for spiritual rest.

Carl's death was another defining moment for me. Martin Luther is said to have noted there are two days in life: today and *that day*. Everything we do today needs to be focused on *that day*. *That day* to which Luther was referring is the judgment seat of Christ, when each of us as a believer will stand before Christ and be asked to give an account of our life.

I find many of us are consumed by plans for tomorrow. "I'll get committed to Christ *tomorrow*," we might say. "I'll get serious about my faith *tomorrow*." Or we say, "I'm really going to do what I know my Lord wants me to do *tomorrow*." "I'll tell Carl about Jesus *tomorrow*."

But then somehow *tomorrow* never comes. But *that day* will come! And suddenly we will be standing before Jesus, and He'll say, "Okay, John, give me an account of how you spent your time on earth." Imagine if all I can manage to say at that point is, "Well, Jesus, You know, I really planned to get serious about it *tomorrow*." He would have every right to say, "John, you said that for thirty years, and *tomorrow* never came. I'm so disappointed in you!"

I felt humiliation after Carl died. My friend's death was a hard way to learn that obeying God always means obeying Him *today*. It means saying, "Yes, Lord, no matter what—*and no matter when!*" I learned a painful lesson. And thank God for the forgiveness we have in Christ. God is certainly bigger than I am as it relates to Carl and what his needs were. But I learned not to postpone obedience. When God asks me to speak or to act, I need to do it right then—tired body or not.

Carl's death showed me just how little separates today from *that day*. And before I would leave Vietnam, I personally would brush up against that razor-thin barrier.

Chapter 14

UNLESS GOD
ALLOWS IT

"I have found that if I go as far as I can, God often opens up the rest of the way." — Isobel Kuhn

As I've pointed out, knowing God was ultimately in control over everything that happened on the battlefield freed me from trying to play it safe. My main concern became giving my men every opportunity to hear about and respond to God's love and provision for their salvation in Christ. And so, even though I was a lieutenant, and later a captain, I became very careful about orders involving risk. Risk is unavoidable in combat, but I always felt that knowing Christ meant I had less to lose than the men around me who didn't know Him. I had settled the "what happens when I die?" question; they hadn't. And so I wanted anyone who was open to hearing the answer to that question to have that opportunity.

With this in mind, sometimes I felt more at ease about flanking an ambush myself than asking my men to do it. I had no doubt they would have carried out my orders if I had told them to do it. But I didn't want to see any of them killed, especially since they didn't know Jesus. As I say, I was free in God's hands. But I wanted my men to hear and respond to the message of the gospel before they died. The incident with Carl had taught me a lot about not putting opportunities to share Christ off until later.

I suppose some people reading these stories may think I had gone crazy. My wife, Susie, was certainly beginning to wonder. And who could blame her? After our first year of marriage, I had been gone for most of the next two years. We started out as just two young college kids. She, especially, was catching the brunt of a very immature young man. I had done nothing to prepare her for my absence after being shipped out. Now I was writing to her on pieces of cardboard or whatever I could find during down times, telling her about "Jesus this, and Jesus that." This new person she was hearing from had to be a stranger to her, as she had no way to gauge what was happening inside of him. Not surprisingly, she would write back, "I don't know who you are! You're not the guy I married." Looking back on it now, I can understand her reaction. She was right: I was a long way from the "up and down" guy I'd been during the first year or so of our marriage. Fortunately, as He always does, God had a better plan for my reentry than I did.

With less than a week to go in my tour of duty, our company was once again ordered into the hot zone. According to policy, I was not supposed to be part of that operation, since I was getting ready to go home and be discharged from the service. But as I've explained, my thought was, "Hey, we've got guys here who are not ready to put themselves into that kind of risk. They're not ready to die and face eternity. I am." So I volunteered for the mission.

When we arrived on the scene, another company had already set up a base of operation with a secure perimeter. The plan was to spend the night there and then go out into the surrounding area on the next day and sweep it of any Vietcong.

As night fell, I decided to hang out near the command post. I sat down on a C-rations cart so I could look up at the sky. It was another one of those amazingly clear nights, with the stars just on fire, twinkling and sparkling. The beauty and majesty of it all was beyond description. I began worshiping the Lord, with passages like Psalm 19:1 welling up in my heart: "The heavens declare the glory of God; the skies proclaim the work of his hands" (NIV). I probably spent an hour or so just sitting there, having a great time with the Lord.

Then the cart broke! Next thing I knew, I was lying on the ground, rather rudely brought back to the current situation. As I picked myself up, I thought, *Well, I need to get some sleep. We've got an operation tomorrow.* So I walked around in front of the command bunker and went to bed.

I'd been lying there for maybe five or ten minutes when, all of a sudden, the night erupted into chaos. Gunfire exploded. Bullets started flying. Someone in the bunker shouted, "Here they come! Here they come! They're coming!" I jumped up. But before I even had time to move—*boom!* I took a hit to my right leg and collapsed back on the ground. I started crawling, trying to get around to the opening of the bunker.

I never found out exactly what happened that night, whether the enemy had launched a full-scale assault on our position, or whether the battle was just a sporadic firefight. But with blood pouring out of my leg, I was pretty much out of it. The first responders began shooting me full of morphine to try and kill the pain and keep me from going into shock.

While we waited for a chopper to transport me out of there, my commanding officer—the one whose orders I had more or less disobeyed by carrying the wounded V-C out of the jungle—stayed by my side. "Hang in there, John," he kept telling me. "We're gonna get you out of here. Hang on, buddy."

RADICAL TRUST

My CO had never made an issue over the incident with the V-C. In fact, to my surprise and great encouragement, he later recommended that I be awarded the Bronze Star Medal for Valor for my actions in an earlier operation. When I learned I would be receiving the nation's fourth highest combat award for the Armed Forces, I was deeply grateful to him for that consideration.

I had tried to talk to him about Christ on several occasions, but he was never interested. Now, with my leg bleeding profusely, and showing obvious signs that I was drifting into shock, he clearly looked worried as to whether or not I would make it.

For whatever reason, I happened to have a pocket version of the Gospel of John on me. So I pulled it out and waved it in front of him. "Okay," I said, "I need one commitment from you. Tell me you'll read this book."

Naturally, he wanted to be accommodating: "Yes, yes, yes! I'll read it!"

But I was insistent. "You promise me you'll read it?"

"Yeah, yeah, yeah! I'll read it!"

Then, the chopper arrived. They loaded me on. I never saw my CO again, and never found out whether he followed through on his promise to read the Gospel of John. But I think here's where God's amazing sovereignty takes over. We can never know how God will use the ripple effects of our faltering efforts to tell people about Him. But we have His assurance that "my word that goes out from my mouth. . .will not return to me empty, but will accomplish what I desire and achieve the purpose for which I sent it" (Isaiah 55:11, NIV).

Chapter 15

GOD MEANT IT FOR GOOD

"The surest affliction never appears intolerable except when we see them in the wrong light." — Brother Andrew

There was another Marine lying in a stretcher above mine in the chopper, who had also been shot. Later I learned my fellow officers figured out the bullet that hit him was probably the same bullet that hit me.

Whatever the case, gangrene set in on my leg. Later that night, as the medical personnel were preparing to operate on me back at base camp, I got rather forceful with them about what they were planning to do. I was all drugged up as they were trying to put me under for the surgery. But they couldn't get me under, because I was too keyed up and out of it mentally.

RADICAL TRUST

I kept telling them, "Guys, don't take my leg! Do not cut my leg off!" They nodded and gave me some more anesthetic. But that only made me more emphatic: "Do not cut my leg off!" (As you can see, I still had a ways to go on truly accepting the loss of an arm or a leg if that was God's best for me—never mind the fact that I was loaded up on morphine!)

The medics were getting frustrated with me. I remember them saying, "We can't get him under! He won't go down!"

About that time I raised myself on the gurney and grabbed the surgeon by his shirt. "Don't you cut my leg off!"

He was startled, but said, "Okay, okay, okay!"

I knew he would do whatever was necessary for my health and safety. But I wanted him to know in no uncertain terms, if at all possible, I wanted to come out of the operation with both legs.

Eventually, of course, they got me under and did whatever they needed to do. Fortunately, they left my leg intact! Then they transported me to the Philippines. I underwent more surgery there. I recuperated for four or five days. Ultimately they shipped me to Corpus Christi, Texas, to a rehab hospital at a naval air station. Susie was living in Dallas, so she came down.

And that was how God used my injury for good. Getting shot was awful, but coming back home on a stretcher allowed a gentler reentry with Susie than I otherwise would have had. As I indicated earlier, we desperately needed that transitional time. I can only imagine what might have happened to our marriage had I come charging out of the Marines as a fired-up Christian, like a bull in a china closet. I have no doubt I would have made every mistake in the book. But forced to spend several weeks in the hospital, I had a chance to get reacquainted with my wife more slowly, and to lay a more solid foundation for the relationship. It was gracious of God to give us that time. We got to spend about a year just getting to know one another while I was recuperating. Today, praise God, I'm pleased to report in January 2011 Susie and I celebrated our fiftieth wedding anniversary.

What's Next?

As I began to think about getting my discharge from the military and reentering civilian life, the big question was: *What do I do with my life?*

I guess most people just pick a field and go into it. But it wasn't that easy for me. I was burning to tell people my story about what I had discovered about Jesus' love and my experience with Him. My relationship with Christ wasn't just theory for me. I mean, Jesus and I had been through the war together! We'd gone through firefights together. He was right there with me when I took that bullet. I couldn't just switch that off when I came back home. So even when I was recuperating in the hospital, I looked for every opportunity to tell people about Jesus.

For instance, while I was recovering I was assigned to the Advocate General, the legal department of the Marine Corps. They would send me out to gather evidence. I would be interviewing a guy taking his testimony, and I'd turn the conversation toward spiritual things with the statement: "Let me tell you how you can know God personally." Since I was an officer, the man would reply, "Yes, sir!" He more or less had to listen to me.

My options for my next steps seemed to boil down to three: go into business, go to seminary to prepare for the ministry, or join a ministry without going to seminary.

The seminary question became an easy call. After Susie and I moved back to Dallas, someone introduced me to Dr. Howard Hendricks at Dallas Theological Seminary (DTS). I asked him if I could sit in on some of his classes. "Why, certainly!" he replied with his characteristic enthusiasm. So I visited DTS two or three times to get a feel for seminary training. I loved Prof. Hendricks's teaching, but it didn't take me long to realize seminary was not for me.

Following my exposure to seminary, I decided to go into the business world. Except I set up my business model in a way that would allow me to do business with about 50 to 60 percent of my time, and do ministry with the rest. I went into investments—real estate, and oil and gas. I worked hard, but it was clearly through God's blessing that I did well, especially given that I was working only on a part-time basis.

RADICAL TRUST

My business involved deal-making, but I was never a deal junkie. I'd do a deal and make enough for my family and me to live on for a year or so. This work allowed me to spend the rest of my time hanging out at places where I could meet people, like on the campus of Southern Methodist University. Hayden Fry was the football coach in those days, and with my background in football, I made his acquaintance. Before long, he had me coming out as a chaplain to work with the football players. I also showed up at the student union two or three days a week in order to engage college students in conversations about Jesus.

As I got older, people invited me to start teaching Bible studies. I also began visiting Eastern Europe to work with some people who were doing innovative theological training with pastors and church leaders behind the Iron Curtain (which would soon fall). By the early 1980s, my friends in business started telling me, "Maisel, we'll pay you to get out of the business world! Just go do ministry full-time, and we'll support you." So that's how I ended up full-time in vocational ministry.

In 2 Timothy 2:1-5 (NIV), Paul challenges Timothy to "be strong in the grace that is in Christ Jesus," and he illustrates what that means by describing people in three occupations: the military, sports, and agriculture (which, in that day, amounted to the business world). I've had a taste of all three (as well as vocational ministry). I was an athlete in high school and college, and during my brief stint with the Oilers. I was an officer in the Marines and led men into combat. And I worked for a number of years in the investment field. I discovered the distinct lessons to be learned in all three of those arenas, just as Paul indicated to Timothy. God used my experiences in each one to form my life and, I believe, make me more effective when I finally ended up in vocational ministry.

I especially valued being engaged in the business world, because I now know the potential of what Christ can do there—so long as we actually bring Christ into our work.

Chapter 16

A NEW BATTLEFIELD

"Call upon Me in the day of trouble, I will deliver you,
and you shall glorify Me." — Psalm 50:15

Probably no better venue exists than the workplace for Christians to live out their commitment to Christ. It's the perfect setting for trusting God and saying to Him, "Yes, Lord, no matter what," on the basis He always intends our highest good and that He is sovereign over all and omniscient about it all.

In fact, once I got into the business world, I found it no different than Vietnam in terms of living for Christ. Obviously I didn't have to contend with insects and snakes and people firing bullets at me and laying booby traps. But the challenges spiritually were exactly the same.

Take, for instance, the mind-set that says I have value to the extent that I have superior performance. The business world totally subscribes to that point of view. It tells me *if* I make the sale, or do the deal, or get the funding, or present the more persuasive case, or meet the quarterly targets, or whatever "success" means in my line of work, *then* I'll have standing and be worthy of respect. Like I said earlier, the world's love is conditional love. If–love. I find a lot of believers getting sucked in by that way of thinking.

The performance-based business culture became my new battlefield. It would test whether Christ had really transformed my heart. It was an opportunity to show whether my work was about making an impact for Christ, or just making a buck.

And I'll be honest, it was hard! I had to fight with my heart on a daily basis to keep saying, "Yes, Lord, no matter what." It was just like the old hymn says: "Prone to wander, Lord, I feel it, prone to leave the God I love."[1] My spiritual fight was exactly as it had been in Vietnam. In Nam I had to come to the point where what mattered was not whether I lived or died, but whether God's glory was honored. So in the business world I had to come to the point where I didn't care whether the deal got done or not. The issue was glorying God and accomplishing His purposes. God would be glorified through the integrity of the process. And if, because of me, the guy I was working the deal with was confronted in some way with Jesus, be it in word or in deed, God was pleased.

Make no mistake, I worked hard and with a good work ethic. I prepared. I honed my approach. I analyzed the financials. I studied my competition. I put in the hours. I paid the price everyone else does to be as successful in business as I could be. But in the end, I knew it was God who would decide whether to bless my work.

Therefore, the whole point: It was God who was superintending my path. Not any sort of brilliant performance on my part. It was God Himself— the God who loves me perfectly and allows nothing to touch my life except what brings about my highest good. God being perfectly loving and sovereign was right there beside me in every transaction, in every conversation, in every circumstance. This God-confidence gave me a freedom that most people would regard as recklessness about what would happen in my business. If the guy said yes to my deal, my attitude could be, "Thank You, Lord." And if he said no to the deal, I could still say, "Thank You, Father."

In fact, there were times when I never even got around to talking about the deal. I'd sit down and ask the prospect how he was doing. Then he'd start spilling his guts. Maybe he'd just gotten some bad news from his doctor, or his wife had told him she was leaving him, or his kid was in trouble, or he was facing serious financial problems. Whatever the situation, I'd see whether he was open to letting me talk to him about Jesus. More often than not, he was. And so we'd get deep into conversation about the gospel. And when the time was up, I'd get ready to leave and he'd ask, "Say, John, what was it you wanted to meet with me about?" I would just smile and say, "Oh, that's not important. We can talk about it some other time."

It Doesn't Just Happen

The liberty to do business that way came directly from my experience of God's abiding presence with me. I think in my early days as a believer, God simply graced me with an awareness of Himself. In Vietnam, for instance, I believe He took the initiative to make Himself so real and present to me that I was able to dialog and laugh with Him and worship Him even with incoming rounds zipping past. I wasn't trying to "make" that happen, it was just happening, because God was wrapping me up in His presence in ways that went beyond anything I could comprehend.

As I matured in my faith, I learned I had to become *intentional* about abiding in the Lord's presence. I couldn't just take it for granted. In a similar fashion Moses urged the Israelites to "seek the LORD your God," and then promised them that "you will find Him if you search for Him *with all your heart and all your soul*" (Deuteronomy 4:29, emphasis added).

RADICAL TRUST

In Psalm 27, David says God explicitly told him to "seek My face," to which David responded, "Your face, O Lord, I shall seek" (v. 8).

And in James we are exhorted to "draw near to God and He will draw near to you" (4:8). So even though experiencing God is still a function of His grace, He demands a degree of intentionality on our part about seeking intimacy with Him.

So what does that look like? Well, it probably looks a bit different for each one of us, because we are all unique people, with different personalities and various ways of living life. But for me, one of the means God has used to help me intentionally seek His face is to personalize the Scriptures when I read them. I seek to read the Bible as though Jesus is talking directly to me through the His Word. And for me to talk back to Him.

For instance, say I'm reading 1 Peter 1, where it talks about being "distressed by various trials" and "tested by fire," so that our faith will "result in praise and glory and honor at the revelation of Jesus Christ" (vv. 6–7). I've learned to say, "Okay, Jesus, what do You mean by that? How do You test my faith? Are You testing me now? Is there anything in my life that I need to pay attention to because it will *not* result in praise and glory and honor at Your revelation?" The idea is for me to pursue an intentional, personal dialogue with Jesus as I'm digging into His Word.

A similar strategy that seems to help me cultivate intimacy with Christ is to go through the day seeking a sense of His presence and just talking to Him. It's like carrying on an ongoing conversation with the Lord. Like anyone else, I'm still in process learning how to have that conversation on a consistent basis. But I'm trying to be intentional about bringing every situation into the Lord's presence. I'm not trying to "make" something happen, I'm just trying to consciously put myself in a place where Jesus can speak to me if He chooses, because I don't want to go into anything unless Jesus goes with me. It's like Moses said to the Lord at Mount Sinai, "If Your presence does not go with us, do not lead us up from here" (Exodus 33:15).

Let me be clear: God's presence is not a good luck charm for getting the result I want. God's presence *is* the result I want! So back when I was sitting around thinking and dreaming about business deals, I wanted Jesus to be at the forefront of those thoughts and dreams, because that would produce my highest good. (By the way, this would be a great question to ask yourself periodically: *What do you think about when you're by yourself? What do you dream about?* And of course, the key question: *Where is Jesus in relation to where you are?*)

So let's say I was going to someone's office to make a presentation about a business deal. I would consciously talk to Jesus about that presentation. I'd say something like, "Jesus, thank You for letting me talk with this person. I don't know what the outcome is going to be, but if You're asking me, I would love it if You'd give me favor with him. But Jesus, whatever this guy decides to do, I want to thank You in advance for his decision, whether he says yes or he says no."

Basically, I was trusting that God was in sovereign control over my deal, and over the conversation, and over the impact of that conversation on my deal. God knew all about my financial needs, as well as my needs as a man for respect and being able to provide for my family. In addition, God knew what I couldn't know, which is His ultimate purpose in everything that touches me and how it all fits into His plan for the world.

So you see, His presence freed me up from thinking that everything depended on me trying to portray a dashing personality, or trying to have an attractive appearance, or trying to make a brilliant presentation. Yes, I worked hard to show up prepared and to pursue my work with a standard of excellence. But ultimately I knew God was the One I could trust to bring about the best outcome for me.

Endnote

[1] Robert Robinson, "Come, Thou Fount of Every Blessing," originally in *A Collection of Hymns Used by the Church of Christ in Angel Alley, Bishopgate* (1758).

Chapter 17

FIGHTING FOR INTIMACY
WITH JESUS

"Wash your face every morning in the bath of praise."
— Charles Spurgeon

When I say trusting God set me "free," I'm maybe understating the reality of that: in truth, trusting God at times has made me *carefree*, almost to a fault! I can recall various times when I was behind the Iron Curtain, and the authorities would take me aside into an interrogation room and demand to know what I was "really" doing in their country. I'd just say, "Well, let me explain why I'm here. I'm here to tell your people how they can have a personal relationship with God." Naturally, that produced some pretty odd looks on their faces. Most of them didn't know what to do with that, because they were coming from an atheistic perspective.

So I'd continue: "May I have your permission to tell you what I'm getting ready to say to the people in your country?"

Usually they'd reply, "Oh, yes, yes, yes!" So I'd give them the gospel. It was an amazing freedom I had in the Lord to take risks, knowing that God would work out whatever happened to His glory.

I think such freedom is a gift of God's grace. A person can't just conjure that up through their own efforts. And in my case, it wasn't because I was somehow more disciplined or more committed than other believers. Hogwash! It was simply God's graciousness to me. But having this viewpoint, I also know God's presence is so imperative that I can't afford not to be intentional about seeking it and even fighting for it, so as to respond to His gracious willingness to have an intimate relationship with me.

The struggle to stay intimate with Jesus is a daily, moment-by-moment fight. And yesterday's successes have nothing to do with today's battles. It doesn't matter how close to Jesus I was thirty years ago, or last year, or even earlier this week. Every day is a new day, with new challenges. It's similar to combat in Vietnam: just because we won a firefight one day has no bearing on the firefight we had to face the next day. So it is with Jesus. Every spiritual battle is a new test of trust.

The Christians I worry about the most are the ones who've seen some victory in their walk with Christ, and then they start coasting. The telltale sign of coasting is that someone can tell you about the great thing Christ did in their life in the past, but they never talk about what He did just yesterday, or what He did this morning, or even what He's doing right now.

Indeed, the greatest enemy for much of the church in the United States today is believers who started out in a vital, growing relationship with the Lord have, over time, become spiritually content in the condition in which they are. They are like cars that have shifted into "park." The engine may still be running, but they're sitting idle, going nowhere.

Somehow those folks have forgotten there are only two gears in the Christian life: We're either engaged in "drive" and moving forward, or we've put it in "reverse" and we're going backwards. We're either moving toward Christ or away from Him. And so if someone is just coasting along, they are actually retreating. Jesus didn't give us the option of spiritual contentment. He's never going to be a poster child for the status quo. He's always on the offensive, both in the world and in individual lives: taking new territory, bringing grace and freedom to more and more areas of our lives.

In light of following Him, we are called to be intentional about looking for what Jesus is up to in and through us *today* and getting in line with His lead. And yes, there's a sense of constantly pushing the envelope and having a holy dissatisfaction with the way things are. Even when we go through lull periods where it feels as if the Lord has us on the shelf and not a lot is going on spiritually—and those times *will* come—even then, we need to be constantly engaging with Jesus in case He suddenly calls our number: "Lord, I'm waiting for whatever You have for me. I'm preparing for whatever You want to do in the future." He may not use us for a while. In fact, He may choose to never use us again. But if and when He does send us into the game, we had better have been preparing and not frittering our time away on idle preoccupations.

Good Is the Enemy of the Best

I can't stress enough how susceptible we affluent Christians in America are to spiritual contentment. A lot of it has to do with the fact that we are surrounded by so many good things. Not bad things—*good things!* Most of the men I've worked with over the past forty years are successful businessmen. They're not struggling to sober up and find their way from the gutter to the soup kitchen. Nor are they looking over their shoulder to see if a cop is going to arrest them for robbing a bank. No, their struggles are mostly with good things no one can really call sin.

For example, a guy will ask me, "John, I've got a house in Dallas, a house in Orange County, a cabin in Colorado, and a lake house in East Texas. Do you think I'm spending too much money on things?" How do I respond? You can't say owning a house is wrong. You can't even say owning two houses is sin. If anything, you could argue that having various homes around the country could be a good thing, in that it gives that person lots of places to spend time with his family. Plus he can use those homes to bless other people who need places to retreat and rest. And of course, there's always the investment angle.

In truth, I would never tell a man how much to give or how much to spend. It's better for him to wrestle with the Lord about such specifics. But I would always tell him whatever he does, he will someday give an account to God.

And so I might challenge him to pray the prayer of Agur in Proverbs 30:8–9: "Give me neither poverty nor riches; feed me with the food that is my portion, that I not be full and deny You and say, 'Who is the LORD?' or that I not be in want and steal, and profane the name of my God."

In the end, it doesn't matter whether it's houses or golf or even grand-kids—the question is: Is there *anything* distracting us from intimacy with Jesus? Is there *anything* moving our hearts away from Him, instead of toward Him?

The longer someone has been a believer, the more ruthless they have to be in answering that question. Or rather I should say, the more attentive they need to be in listening for the voice of the Holy Spirit as He puts His finger on any area of divided loyalties.

Not long ago, I was sitting in church one Sunday as the noon hour approached. The preacher was going over his allotted time in the service. So instead of paying attention to what he was saying, I was thinking, *You need to shut this thing down, buddy! The Cowboys game starts at noon. Don't make me miss the kickoff!* Fortunately, he landed the plane just shy of 12:00, and the closing hymn was brief. So before the pastor had even said the "amen" to his benediction, I was up the aisle, out the door, into my car, and tuned in to the game. I was totally into the game.

It was at that moment that I heard the Lord asking me, "John, have you made this football game an idol?" I was shocked! "Idol" is a strong word. Yeah, maybe I was a bit impatient in getting to the car. But really—football as an idol?! But the Lord wouldn't let me rest: "John, has your heart given more importance to this game than to Me?" Before long I had to stop and confess that it had!

Now someone might ask, "Well, how is tuning in to a football game a sin?" And the answer is, it's not. It's not a sin in and of itself. But the sin has to do with my heart. *Anything*—even a good thing, even a thing that is not inherently sinful—can become a sinful idol if it comes between my Lord and me. And at this stage in my life, and in my relationship with Christ, most of my sinful idols come from *good* things that distract me from the *best* thing, which is Jesus.

What Jesus Really Wants

Even ministry can distract us from Jesus! Such a statement is hard for a lot of sincere Christian people to believe. Because there's a mind-set in the church that if you're *really* serious about your faith, if you're *really* serious in your commitment to Christ, then you'll quit your "secular" job and go do "full-time" vocational ministry. You'll become a minister or a missionary or work with a nonprofit Christian organization. The idea is if you're doing kingdom work, *then* you'll have a great relationship with the King.

Let me respond, first by saying *every* believer is called to serve the King, no matter what he or she does for work. And the only job that matters to God is the one He calls you to pursue. If He calls you into ministry, you'd better go into ministry and minister to the glory of God. But if He calls you into business, or law, or medicine, or education, or government, or home-making, or any other occupation, you better go into that area and do such work to the glory of God.

But even more to the point: If you think doing ministry is what Jesus cares about, you obviously don't understand the heart of the King. *What Jesus is after is our intimacy with Him, not our ministry for Him.*

I honestly believe this truth is the single biggest reason why God allows us to hit low points whenever we try to accomplish great things for Him. We get all excited about our initiatives to reach the world and save the lost and make great strides for the kingdom. We're full of vim and vigor as we launch out to further God's purposes. We're all in! But then come the hard times. We hit roadblocks. We lose funding. People disappoint us. They quit and go away. Every idea we had turns into nothing. Pretty soon we're sitting there with the ruins of our dream scattered around us like so much trash. We start to wonder: Did we miss God's call?

God allows us to get to that point so that we finally realize His call is first and foremost and always about our heart. *The call is to intimacy with Him,* not doing things for Him. For that reason, He waits for us to reach a point where we look at the mess we're in and say, "Wow, it sure hasn't worked out the way we thought it was going to work out! But Lord, we know we're here at You're calling. And Lord, it's okay. Whatever is necessary for You to be honored and glorified, it's okay, Father. And we're just going to continue a life of faith, and to trust You."

When we get to that point, then God says, "Now I've got My person!"

You see, it's all about trusting the Lord, no matter what happens. It's not about what He's going to do through us, or about His blessings. It's about intimacy with Jesus. Once Jesus has our hearts, He can begin to fulfill the ministry and the purposes He initially laid on our hearts.

Chapter 18

ABANDONED TO LOVE

"Except you become like a child. . ." — Mark 10:15 (paraphrase)

Intimacy with Christ sets us free from worrying what will happen if we follow through on doing what Christ asks us to do. I'm reminded of my beautiful granddaughter, Nicole. When she was in the third grade, Susie and I were invited to Grandparents' Day at her school. We were delighted for the opportunity to see her work and meet her teachers. At one point, one teacher had all of us gather in front of a bulletin board. The kids had cut out silhouettes of themselves and then written something about their family underneath their silhouette. The grandparents had to guess which silhouette matched to their grandchild. We found this to be easy because underneath Nicole's silhouette she had written, "I obey my parents because I know they love me and I trust them."

Bingo! Confidence in a parent's love results in trust, and trust results in obedience. If Christians today could ever embrace this kind of simple, childlike faith in our relationship with our heavenly Father, God's glory would fall upon us and His joy would dance like a flag over our hearts!

Remarkably, Jesus said it's not difficult to have such faith. One time His disciples asked Him to increase their faith, but Jesus replied that it wasn't the size of their faith that mattered. It was the presence of faith, period (see Luke 17:5–6). It's a simple, childlike trust that Nicole expressed: a confidence in her parents' love.

From history, a noteworthy follower of Christ illustrates this point well. George Müller, the nineteen-century director of the Ashley Down Orphanage in Bristol, England, has been quoted as saying that "ninety percent of understanding the will of God for your life is not really caring what the will of God is."[1] In other words, trust means we come to the point where we say, "Lord, I don't really care what Your will is, just that I'm in Your will—no matter what." There's an abandonment to the outcome of God's will, because there's a confidence about whatever the outcome may be, it will only result in God's glory and our highest good.

So once again we are brought back to our premise:

The depth of our willingness to surrender our hearts to Jesus—to say, "Yes, Lord, no matter what"—is directly related to the depth of our belief that God really loves us with perfect love.

Fatalism Versus Faith

Now when I talk about abandonment to the outcome of God's will, some people may think I'm talking fatalism. Fatalism holds the idea that whatever is going to happen is going to happen, and no one's in control over it—not human beings, not even God. This worldview maintains there's no real purpose to anything, everything just happens by fate.

But my position is based on faith, not fate. Robert Morgan explains that "for Christians, faith is making reasonable assumptions about God's control over our lives, based on His Scriptural promises. . . . Our faith grows when we choose to apply God's promises to today's problems, and use the experience to mature us for tomorrow's challenges."[2] By contrast, fate leaves God out of the equation.

Faith says God has either decreed something to happen or allowed it to happen, even that which I consider evil. God does not initiate evil, but He allows it. And if He allows it, it has purpose. In short, anything that touches my life has purpose. And because God loves me with perfect love, the purpose is always a good purpose, whether or not I see that goodness at the time.

Again, someone might ask, "Okay, John, so when you say that you charged through the jungles of Vietnam with the attitude that 'no bullet can touch me unless God allows it,' how is that any different from the Islamic terrorist who blows himself up with the attitude, 'Whatever Allah wills be done'?"

My response would be that there's really no difference at all in terms of faith being exercised. But the huge difference is the object of faith. The terrorist believes a lie; I was placing my faith in the truth.

You see, what matters is not the intensity of a person's faith, it's the *object* of that faith. It's whether the thing they are putting their faith in turns out to be true. Just because you believe something doesn't make it true. By the same token, just because you don't believe something doesn't make it a lie. The issue is whether it's true regardless of you.

I used to run into this issue behind the Iron Curtain, when I would meet young Marxists who were extremely dedicated to communism. They had great faith. In fact, they had staked their whole lives on the teachings of Marx and Lenin. But they were trusting a lie. It was true faith, but in a false object.

RADICAL TRUST

You can have little faith in the right object, and you're okay. But even if you have great faith, if it's placed in the wrong object, you're in trouble.

So for instance, one man can be scared to death of flying. But if he'll just exercise a teeny-weeny bit of faith and get on a plane that's been properly designed, built, and serviced, the laws of aerodynamics will work in his favor, and he'll fly. His faith is little, but when the plane takes off, its performance doesn't depend on his faith. It will fly.

Meanwhile, another man can come to the airport with all the confidence in the world that flight is possible. He can be totally determined that today is his day to fly. But if he gets in a plane that has a hole in its wing and part of its tail knocked off, he may take off, but it's a 100 percent certainty that he's going to crash.

So in what (or in whom) are you putting your faith?

Endnotes

[1] Adapted from A. Sims, *An Hour with George Mueller* (Grand Rapids, MI: Zondervan, 1939), Appendix C.

[2] Robert Morgan, *The Red Sea Rules* (Nashville: Thomas Nelson, 2001).

Chapter 19

IS YOUR CAUSE WORTH YOUR AFFECTIONS?

"The trust we put in God honors Him much and draws down great grace." — Brother Lawrence

The fact is, all of us are living for something. It's just instinctive for us, as humans, to live for a cause greater than us. You see that all over the world.

One time, while on a plane, I engaged an elderly lady in conversation. I learned she was a university professor with all kinds of advanced degrees in biology, zoology, and ecosystems. She knew her life was drawing to a close. As she advanced in age, she stated a desire to devote the last years of her life to something significant. When I asked her where she was headed, she told me she was going to a protest to save the environment. "I'm hoping I can get arrested one more time before I die," she remarked. I couldn't help but admire her commitment to her cause. I mean, seriously, how many Christians do you know in the United States who would gladly go to jail in order to take a stand for Christ and the gospel?

All of us are living for something. The question is whether or not something is worthy of our deepest affections. Will it capture our highest loyalty? Will it keep us in the fight all the way to the finish? And will it last into eternity?

We're all living for something. The question is whether that something valuable enough that it's not only worth living for, but dying for, as well. Jim Elliot lived to bring the gospel to the Waodani Indians, an indigenous tribe in Ecuador who were locked in bondage to a long history of animism and revenge killings. A lot of people probably thought Elliot was crazy to "waste" his life in the jungles of South America. But he made it very clear what he valued most in life when he wrote in his journal in October 1949: "He is no fool who gives what he cannot keep to gain that which he cannot lose."[1]

A few years later, Elliot and four other missionaries would be killed by the very people they were trying to reach. At the time, the world perceived the loss as a tragedy. But within a few years, Elliot's wife Elisabeth and others brought many of the Waodani to faith—including one of the killers.

Are we living for things that will last into eternity? Again, this is where I worry about men in their 40s and 50s. They're charging along, striving for career success. Then they make it, and by the time they turn 65, the culture says they ought to kick back and start enjoying their "bucket list."

I detest that way of thinking! From my point of view, everything in my life so far has merely been a prologue and a preparation for whatever God has for me next. Frankly, I've asked God that I might bear more fruit in my next five years than I've born in my entire life up to this point, for His glory. But God has the freedom to determine what that looks like. My own idea would be to win millions of people to Christ. If God allowed such a privilege, it would certainly glorify Him.

But on the other hand, His way of glorifying Himself through me might be something very different. It might mean winning just a handful of people to Christ. It might mean becoming disabled and being able just to pray for people to come to Christ. Conceivably it could mean spending most of my time taking care of an invalid family member, where the only time I get out of the house is to go buy groceries.

And you know what? It's okay if that's the best way to give my Lord the glory due Him. Again, I need to get to the point where I pray, "Lord, I don't really care what Your will is—only that I'm in Your will."

So why is winning people to Christ so important to me? In the next chapter I'll explain in greater detail.

Endnote

[1] Elisabeth Elliot, *Shadow of the Almighty: The Life and Testament of Jim Elliot* (London: Hodder and Stoughton, 1958), 15.

Chapter 20

PEOPLE NEED THE LORD

"We must be global Christians with a global vision because our God is a global God." — John Stott

Two things drive my passion for evangelism. The first is I've been around a lot of death. When I was six years old, I saw a guy get murdered. I held him as he breathed his last breath. I've given people mouth-to-mouth resuscitation at airports, only to watch them expire, with their families standing right there. I've gotten off a bus just as a car plowed into a crowd of people, and seen bodies strewn everywhere and heard the wounded screaming. And of course I spent a tour of duty in Vietnam, where I held a lot of men as the life drained out of them.

For most of the Christians I know in America, the deaths they've observed by and large have been the deaths of fellow believers. Even when those deaths have been terribly sad and tragic, there remains a comfort in knowing those people died as believers. But I've watched a lot of unbelievers die. I've seen the moment of the stare, that last sixty seconds before the person slips into a Christ-less eternity. I've heard them cry out in desperation, "Don't let me die, God! Help me, God! Somebody save me! Somebody pray with me!" Those experiences have marked me. Knowing what I know about the love of God and what Christ did to save us from hell, how can I not tell everyone I meet to turn in faith to Jesus, before it's too late?

Peace with God

Scripture says when Christians deal with death, they do grieve, but not like unbelievers who have no hope (1 Thessalonians 4:13). I've seen the contrast time and time again.

Once I helped conduct the funeral of a friend by the name of Ron Plyler who died of cancer at the relatively young age of 50. There were surely feelings of sadness and loss in that church as we said "goodbye" to our brother. But Ron comforted all of us by writing the following letter to be read at the ceremony:

> Several months ago, I had the occasion to stand before you in church and to speak to you about the great lovingkindness of God. At that time, I was judged to be disease-free. I wanted to share my great victory about what God was doing in my life with the many of you who have been praying so diligently through the many months in my behalf. You received that testimony with great joy in your heart, and you all gave glory to God in your applause to Him on my behalf, and because of His great lovingkindness.

Now, as I had been forewarned of the possibilities, the disease has recurred very aggressively. Most of the time they had given me to live has already passed. I now find I am unable to deliver the content of this letter personally.

It occurs to me that some of you might entertain the thought that God has failed me. Please, please, do not let that thought even cross your mind. Because God has not failed me, nor has He failed you who have sustained me through many months of prayers, cards, calls, and many well-wishes. Because I am only dimly able to see God's great strategies from this side of heaven does not constitute any flaw, error, or failure concerning God's best for me. You have been an unbelievable inspiration to me. No, to the contrary, God has not failed me. He has demonstrated to me His lovingkindness even more.

He has taken the fear out of death. He has allowed me to see more of the glory of Himself. He has taken my hand as a loving Father would his young son and calmed all my fears. He has provided circumstances in my life which have magnificently demonstrated His unconditional love and lovingkindness, even the more. I want you to know that God has generated revival in my soul. I want you to know that you've been a part of this supernatural experience that God has led me through. I want you to know that all is well with my soul.

There was a man with hope! Contrast his perspective with a man named Sergey, whom I met in Russia. I had come out of a meeting when a couple of our ministry staff grabbed me and said, "John, there's a man here who says he needs to talk to you."

I asked, "What's the deal?"

They said, "He was a lieutenant colonel in the Russian army when they were in Afghanistan, and he committed a lot of atrocities there. Now he's a mafia hit man, and he just carried out an execution. Except he killed the wrong guy, so now both the mafia and the police are after him. He says he'll only talk to someone who has been in combat."

So that was how I was introduced to Sergey. He was sitting in a room with a bunch of bodyguards around him, hiding out. The next couple of days were incredible as we talked about his situation. He was terribly plagued by fears and by all of the images in his mind relating to choices he had made and things he had done in Afghanistan.

I'll never forget when Sergey looked across the table at me and asked, "John, do you fear death?" It was clear he did. He was terrified of what is on the other side of death.

I said, "No, Sergey, I don't fear death."

He said, "Why? Why don't you fear death?"

"Because I have peace with God," I told him.

At that moment he rose up, reached right across the table, and grabbed my arm. Then, beating his chest, he cried out in a frenzied voice, "Peace with God! Peace with God! Oh, help me find peace with God!"

Do you realize at least 5 billion of the 6.5 billion people in this world are crying out for the same peace with God that Sergey gave voice to? Most of them have lived very different lives from Sergey. But their anguish to find peace with God is exactly the same. Eventually every one of them will die, and as they come to death, they fear it because they instinctively know they are not at peace with God. They are desperate to find hope.

I don't know how anyone who truly knows the love, grace, forgiveness, and peace that are to be found only in Jesus can avoid reaching out to those desperate people with the good news of the gospel.

One Afternoon in Romania

The second thing that fuels my zeal to proclaim the gospel—and something that should drive every Christian in the West to actively share the good news of Jesus with others—is the countless followers of Christ around the world who are suffering for their faith. Talk about being "all in" for God! Some of our brothers and sisters have given up *everything* for His sake and the sake of the gospel. For them it's not Jesus *plus* a comfortable lifestyle, or Jesus plus social status, or Jesus *plus* a group of friends, or Jesus *plus* anything. It's just Jesus. Jesus *plus nothing!* They place themselves entirely in the hands of Jesus with a no strings attached trust that says, "Jesus, I will do whatever You ask of me—no matter what!"

Allow me to illustrate. Earlier I mentioned in the 1980s I started working with pastors and church leaders in Eastern Europe. Some of my friends in the United States thought I was taking considerable risks in going behind the Iron Curtain. What if the communist authorities discovered my activities? What if I were arrested? I certainly weighed those risks and took precautions accordingly. But in the end, the worst that could happen to me would be deportation and perhaps an order to never return to the country.

However, the risks to the Eastern European Christians were far more serious. One time in Romania, for example, I was supposed to meet a man who would take me to a group of believers. I waited for more than hour, but my contact never showed. Later I learned he had been arrested just before our scheduled rendezvous. A search of his car had uncovered a few pieces of Christian literature. He had been quickly sent off to prison.

I pondered that man's outcome on different occasion as I stood on another street in Romania, waiting for a similar rendezvous. I tried to appear inconspicuous, which was hard to do since the street was practically deserted. Furthermore, it was late afternoon in the middle of winter. So what was I doing standing outside a storefront, shivering in the relentless, bitterly cold wind?

I made sure the postcard I was clutching was completely visible, so my contact would know who I was, once he arrived. But he was late, and I had to resist the urge to check my watch again, even though I was certain I was in the right spot, at the right time, on the right day.

Then suddenly I was aware of a figure standing a few yards away. He was a man. He seemed to have come out of nowhere. He stood in front of the shop, gazing through the window at the merchandise, paying no attention to me. But my heart leaped up when I saw that he, too, held a postcard in his left hand.

After a moment he lifted his head slightly and our eyes met for a fraction of a second. Then he quickly turned and began walking away. I breathed a silent prayer of thanks, and then counted slowly to ten before I began following him.

He led me down various streets. I was careful to maintain a fair distance. I knew better than to look over my shoulder, but it wasn't long before I caught a glimpse of another man following me, just as I'd expected. His job was to ensure I hadn't been followed. So far, so good.

The three of us blended in well with the handful of pedestrians who were on the streets. There was a sameness about those people that was eerie to me: all heads bent, all eyes downcast, all figures bundled up in shabby, bulky clothing, all expressions cheerless. What sorts of things went through their minds as they shuffled through the grayish slush? Did they ever get "used to" living under the heel of communist oppression? Surely somewhere inside they must have felt a yearning for a better way, and for freedom. But how many of them actually knew there is a God, or that Jesus had come as the Light of the world?

We rounded yet another corner, and then I looked up to find my guide standing at the end of the block, facing me. He was motioning urgently for me to hurry as a small, battered car was pulling up to the curb beside him. I broke into a run as my contact opened the back door of the car. I dove in and the door slammed shut. We sped off, passing my companion who had already returned to his shuffled walk down the street, as if nothing had happened.

I breathed a sigh of relief, and then turned to look at the man who was sitting next to me in the back seat. He had a big grin on his face and a joyful twinkle in his eye. He let out a low, growling laugh. His amusement was infectious, and I began laughing, too. We clasped hands as if we were longtime friends, and just nodded. It was the only way we could communicate, but it was enough.

The car wound through the streets of the city for a while, making frequent turns to make sure we were not being followed. Then, as the dusk retreated into real darkness, we pulled clear of the city altogether. After about an hour of bouncing along rural roads, the car slowed to a crawl, and the driver killed the headlights. It was pitch-black outside. I couldn't imagine how the driver could navigate in such darkness. But eventually we came to a stop. Our car flashed its headlights three times, and in the brief flickers I realized we had come to a large wooden gate.

The gate slowly swung open as the car moved forward in total darkness. A large house—large by Romanian standards—loomed ahead. When the car rolled to a stop, my companion and I got out and quietly stepped up onto the porch. We didn't say a word. Then the front door opened and a shadowy figure hurried us inside. The house was completely dark and utterly silent.

Instinctively I stretched out my hand to brush the coat of the man in front of me. He began moving forward. I felt as if I were in some strange dream as we took baby steps, hugging the wall and taking care not to trip over anything or knock something over. At last we passed through a doorway and came to a stop. I sensed more than heard the slight rustling and steady breathing that indicated a lot of people were nearby. I heard a door close. Then, after a moment's pause, the flick of a switch flooded the room with light.

I was startled, of course, having adjusted my eyes to the utter blackness outside. But the transformation of the mood inside was instantaneous. More than thirty people were in front of me, some sitting in chairs, others on the floor, all beaming with smiles, chuckling, nodding, and gesturing to welcome me into their presence.

I already knew they had made great efforts and even sacrifices to be there. Some had walked long distances, others had likely traveled from afar—even eight hundred miles would not have been unusual. But they had come to hear from God's Word, and their faces were radiant with joy and a sense of gratitude that I had made it to them safely. We could now get started in our fellowship together.

I opened my mouth to say greeting, but nothing came out. I was too overcome with emotion. I was overwhelmed with the realization these believers—persecuted by the authorities and forced to meet in secret— were exactly like the Christians Peter described as "a chosen race, a royal priesthood, a holy nation, a people for God's own possession, that you may proclaim the excellencies of Him who has *called you out of darkness and into His marvelous light*" (1 Peter 2:9, emphasis added).

Yes, even in the dark night of a Romanian winter, even in the spiritual darkness of a country ruled by atheists, the light of the gospel was shining brilliantly. The hope of the world was there, in power. And those dear Christians were eager to learn more about their Savior, so they could proclaim His excellencies to the people in their spheres of influence—those cheerless Romanian people who had no idea there is a better way, a way to true freedom, a way to a good and loving God, a way provided by God's Son, Jesus, the Light of the world.

When I Stand Before Christ

From one point of view, those Romanian Christians were persevering in the midst of considerable suffering. Yet they had a joy and a spirit of thanksgiving that totally outweighed whatever troubles they had to endure. In fact, they didn't come across as people who were suffering, rather they seemed like the happiest people in Romania. For them, it was their loved ones and neighbors who did not know Christ who were suffering—suffering under fear, doubt, confusion, anger, bitterness, selfishness, deceit, cynicism, and all of the other sad outcomes of being lost in sin.

But whether it's in Communist Romania in the 1980s or in capitalist America today, one thing is evident: No one endures suffering for the sake of Christ unless they intimately know Christ. In America, at least, a person can show up to a church service, or donate to Christian causes, or volunteer at a ministry, or even take a mission trip overseas. Surely such activities can have great benefit to one's walk with Christ. But how do those things show that someone knows Christ intimately, in the way He wants to make Himself known to us? Only when there's a real price to pay for following Christ does someone get to show how much they trust in God's perfect love and complete sovereignty.

The apostle Paul's great aspiration was "that I may know [Christ], and the power of His resurrection, *and the fellowship of His sufferings, being conformed to His death*" (Philippians 3:10, emphasis added).

When I read this verse, I visualize my first couple of milliseconds in the presence of Christ. I imagine I've died, and I'm finally standing face-to-face in front of Jesus, my Savior and King. What is that first moment going to be like? Whatever else happens, I know I don't want to be standing there with the feeling of, "Oh, Lord, if only I would have given You what You really wanted of me." Or the feeling of, "Oh, my! I now realize that I never really knew You, Jesus. I trusted in what You did for me on the cross, and that was a good thing. But I never knew You in the way that You wanted to make Yourself known to me."

As the apostle John admonished us, "Little children, abide in Him"— that is, live intimately with Jesus, cultivate a deep, vital relationship with Jesus—"so that when He appears, we may have confidence and not shrink away from Him in shame at His coming" (1 John 2:28).

When we abide in a close, intimate relationship with Christ, it becomes natural and instinctive for us to want others to enter in to that same relationship of intimacy with the Savior. Which of course is exactly what Jesus desires, too. And so, as I indicated in Part I, I believe every encounter we have with another person is actually a divine appointment. The Spirit brings us into contact with others so that when they can interact with us. They interact with Jesus because *we* are in relationship with Jesus. This mind-set doesn't mean we share the gospel with every person we meet, or even that we bring up spiritual issues. But it does mean that every time God brings a person our way, our sensors ought to switch on.

Paul evidenced this sensitivity. He said wherever he and his companions went, "We proclaim [Christ], admonishing *every* man and teaching *every* man with all wisdom, so that we may present *every* man complete in Christ. For this purpose also I labor, *striving* according to His power, which mightily works within me" (Colossians 1:28–29, emphasis added).

God presents us with incredible opportunities to impact people's lives. If we'll just pay attention, we'll often discover that God has already been working behind the scenes; now He's giving us an opportunity to help someone take another step toward Him. Sometimes that step might just be the life-changing one of trusting Christ as Savior.

The Door of Opportunity

So, for example, I once met a man where I work out. He was pretty salty in terms of his language, and at times something of a loudmouth in the locker room. But he was basically a friendly guy, so I joked around with him whenever I ran into him and engaged in social banter. Nothing deep, just developing some rapport. Then one day he walked in, and when I asked how he way doing, he said, "Not real good."

I said, "Really! What's the deal?"

He said, "Well, I just had two buddies of mine die. Guys I worked with, you know, in my career."

I said, "Oh, man, I'm so sorry to hear that."

Well now a door had been opened. This fellow was obviously feeling some pain. The death of his former colleagues had stirred something inside of him. So I pressed into that by saying, "Let me ask you something. Do you think it's possible a person can know before they die what happens next, or whether they go to heaven or not?"

He said, "Absolutely not!"

His response was not an uncommon response to the question I'd asked. It's not necessarily a sign the person isn't open to the gospel. It just means they don't yet see any way to be certain about having peace with God when they die.

So I asked permission to go further by saying, "Well, you know, would you be open to maybe getting together and letting me show you what the Bible says in regards to that?"

Almost with a sense of relief, he said, "Yeah, yeah, I'd be wide open!"

I reached into my gym bag and brought out a little booklet I'd written called, *Is Jesus God?* (which is a brief presentation of the gospel that East–West Ministries uses in our ministry around the world). I handed it to him and said, "Here's something I wrote to kind of develop some of those thoughts. Why don't you read it, and then let's get together for breakfast and talk."

We scheduled a time for the next week, and when he showed up, he was shaking that little booklet in his hand. "I've read through this three times," he excitedly exclaimed. He had it all marked up with passages underlined and questions in the margins. He was very interested in hearing how a people could know for sure they would go to be with God when they die.

Now that experience of meeting someone in need is very common—not just for me, but for all believers. At least, it is if our spiritual antennae are up and operating. We rub shoulders with people all day long, for months and years at a time—at work, in our neighborhoods, at school (if you're a student), at the gym, at the country club, or wherever. We develop relationships that go beyond just saying "hi." We get to know people; they get to know us.

Then one day, *wham!*, God opens a door of opportunity for a conversation about spiritual matters. If we'll just be sensitive and ask nonthreatening questions, we might be amazed at where the conversation goes. We'll often discover God has been at work in the person's life, and now we have an opportunity to help him or her take another step toward

Him. But we don't have to push it. If we throw out an opening question and the person runs with it, fine. If not, that's fine, too. No matter what happens, we can trust that God is at work.

God Is *Always* at Work

Let me repeat: *No matter what happens,* God is at work. We have to hold onto that, because sometimes we'll get rejected or whatever, and unless we're trusting God's sovereignty, we may just give up.

For instance, on another occasion Susie and I were at a party. We were talking with a small group of people when this guy came along and joined the conversation. I'd interacted with him some before, so he kind of knew where I was coming from as a believer. The group was discussing a spiritually related topic. I was offering my perspective out of my convictions regarding Christ.

Well, this fellow had had a bit too much to drink. So suddenly he blurted out right there in front of the group, "Maisel, I think Jesus Christ was an SOB!"

Now that was a direct challenge! Not to me, but to the gospel. I must admit, I hadn't seen it coming. But somehow God gave me the presence of mind to just smile and say, "Oh? You know, that is really an interesting observation. I've never heard that before."

Now he was the one who was looking surprised. I said, "I'm sure you've done some research to come to that conclusion. You know, I'd love to get together with you and talk about how you arrived at that conclusion."

When he realized his sarcastic jab had not had its intended effect, he just waved his hand and walked off. The others in the group shook their heads, and the group kind of dispersed. But as we were walking away, one of the guys who had witnessed this exchange grabbed my elbow and quietly said, "Hey, listen, I'd like to get together with you and talk about this stuff." A week later that man trusted Christ as his Savior.

We *have* to realize God is at work. Everywhere! All the time! We usually don't see Him in action. Not until just the right moment when He brings us into the story and we play our "bit part" in His larger purposes.

Another way to say this is: *We live with certainty of God's love, but uncertainty of God's plan.* We can never fully know what God is up to. But we can always be confident that whatever He is up to involves an infinitely good purpose.

Chapter 21

GOD IS NOT BOUND
TO A CLOCK

"I know He tries me only to increase my faith, and that all in love. Well, if He is glorified, I am content." — Hudson Taylor

Much of our struggle with accepting uncertainty regarding God's plan is our clocks and God's clock are almost never in sync. For instance, when we pray and make some request of God, we tend to expect Him to answer our prayer fairly quickly, if not immediately. What we don't see is that in answering our prayers, God often will do things far beyond what we have asked.

So, for example, when we ask Him to heal a loved one who is sick, He may eventually answer the request. But He also may do a lot more: He may do it in a way that causes our faith to grow; causes His name to be glorified before others; causes the loved one to gain a deeper sense of His presence; causes other people to pray; causes us to get into His Word more; causes us to reevaluate our values; or countless other possibilities. Those good outcomes exceed what we ever asked for, but most of them take time to occur.

God will always bring about His good purposes, but always according to His timing, not ours. He is not bound to our clocks or schedules.

The classic illustration of this truth may be found with Abraham. God promised Abraham a son when he was seventy-five years old. This possibility may sound like a stretch! But twenty-five years later, Abraham was still waiting for God to make good on His promise. Romans 4 tells us Abraham "contemplated his own body, now as good as dead since he was about a hundred years old, and the deadness of [his wife] Sarah's womb" (v. 19). In other words, the circumstances seemed to contradict the promise of God. What might have been remotely possible twenty-five years before was now totally out of the question.

But there's a reason why Abraham is called the father of faith: "In hope against hope he believed. . . . [With] respect to the promise of God, he did not waver in unbelief but grew strong in faith, giving glory to God, and being fully assured that what God had promised, He was able also to perform" (4:18, 20-21).

I love the way *The King James Bible* renders that passage: "He staggered not at the promise of God through unbelief; but was strong in faith." Abraham didn't give up, because he trusted God—*not the circumstances*. He remained certain of God's love, even if he was uncertain of God's plan.

Not long ago I was talking with a colleague from Asia with whom we've been working for the past twenty-five years. His country does not allow the gospel to be proclaimed freely, so needless to say it's been a long, hard road for him in his work of evangelism and church-planting. In light of all the hardship he endured, especially in his early years, he often wanted to give up and go do something else. Many of us prayed with him and for him, that God would give him the strength to persevere and, in time, reward his faithfulness. Just within the past few months, this man has seen more fruitful results from his labors than he ever thought possible. I recently asked him, "Aren't you glad that you didn't quit?"

Our Steps Are Directed By God

Proverbs 16:9 says, "The mind of man plans his way, but the LORD directs his steps." Likewise, Jeremiah 10:23 says, "LORD, I know that people's lives are not their own; it is not for them to direct their steps" (NIV).

I learned the truth of those passages firsthand in Vietnam. A constant problem as we went out on patrol was booby traps. We might go out three or four days at a time and never engage the enemy directly, yet we still incurred numerous casualties from booby traps. The V-C laid them everywhere.

So it was very comforting to know every step I took was a step God in His sovereignty and love was directing and overseeing. In effect, He had gone before me and knew exactly where my feet needed to land.

I recall a couple of times when I stepped on booby traps that had just a small space between the trigger and the trap. My foot came down exactly between them so that I did not trigger the trap. Another kind of trap that I narrowly avoided was made of "punji sticks," sharply pointed bamboo spikes designed to cause severe injury and slow a unit down.

Why I never tripped off a booby trap while others with me did is not because I was a Christian and they were not. To say God was "directing my steps" does not mean God was somehow "looking out for me" such that I would never get injured. The bullet I took in my leg is evidence enough of my vulnerability. No, Christian soldiers stepped on booby traps in Vietnam, and non-Christian soldiers avoided them.

If anything, that only validates the truth of Proverbs 16 and Jeremiah 10: *God directs everyone's steps.* We can't fully explain His ways. They largely remain a mystery. Why He takes one person one way and another person another way is not given us to know. All we are told is He is God, and His ways are different from the ways we might choose.

RADICAL TRUST

Thirty Years to Make an Eternal Decision

Not long ago I was experiencing some problems with my leg whenever I ran. So one day I went for a massage at my fitness center. The fellow working on my leg remarked, "My gosh! Where did you get that scar?"

"Oh, I got shot in Vietnam," I told him.

"Is that right?" he replied. "You know, I had a friend of mine who got really messed up in Vietnam."

"What happened?" I asked.

"Oh, he got both his legs blown off. Terribly sad!"

I asked him, "What service was he in?"

"Marine Corps."

"Really?" I shot back. Since I was in the Marines, he really had my curiosity going. "When was he there?"

"About '67, '68."

That's when I was there. So I asked, "What was his name?"

"Jim Husbeth," he told me.

With his answer I came right off the table. "Jim Husbeth!" He nodded. The name Jim Husbeth was one I could never forget. "Let me tell you the story of Jim Husbeth," I exclaimed.

I told the masseuse how my men and I were in a blackout aboard a ship off the Vietnamese coast, getting ready to go into a hot spot the next day. I walked out on the back of the ship, and there was a Marine standing guard there. So I went up and struck up a conversation. His name was Jim Husbeth.

After a while I began telling Jim about God's love for him, and that God had a purpose and plan for his life. Eventually I asked if he wanted to trust Jesus as his Savior. Jim said he'd have to think about that offer. But we had a good conversation back and forth. Finally I said, "Hey, listen, I've got an operation tomorrow. I gotta turn in. I hope to see you sometime."

"I'd like that," Jim replied.

The next day we went out on patrol. I had the point platoon, as we came up on a hill. The Vietcong had left, but they had booby-trapped the site pretty heavily. So I called back to the main unit and told the officers in charge we needed to sweep the hill of the traps. I said I'd call them back when we had finished cleaning them out.

My men and I formed a skirmish line, and we moved very slowly and cautiously as we looked for traps. Somehow I got out in front of the line, and then I stepped right across an 81-mm mortar booby trap. I planted one foot in front of it and the other foot behind it, just missing stepping right on top of it by taking my natural stride. I took a couple more steps, and then the guy behind me stepped on the trap.

The explosion blew him right up into the air. When he hit the ground, both of his legs were gone. Incredibly, he was still conscious.

Just then the V-C opened up with an ambush, pinning all of us down. But the wounded man was screaming, "Someone help me! Someone pray with me!" I was the closest man to him, so I crawled over beside him and began to pray for him out loud. As soon as he heard my voice, he screamed out, "Lieutenant, I'm the one you talked to about Jesus last night on the ship!" Sure enough, the badly wounded soldier turned out to be Jim Husbeth.

Eventually we suppressed the enemy fire. I was able to radio a chopper in. I stayed with Jim until the medics loaded him in. Then, they took off. I never saw Jim again after that incident. But I never forgot him. I often wondered whether he lived or died.

As I was telling this story to the masseuse, neither one of us had a way of knowing whether the Jim Husbeth he knew was the same Jim Husbeth I had encountered in Vietnam. But it seemed like too much of a coincidence to be otherwise. He offered to try and get the phone number of the man he knew, whom he thought lived in the Northeast, and eventually he did (which was another miracle all in itself).

At any rate, I called the number he gave me, and a man named Jim came on the line.

I began by saying, "I'm not sure whether you're the Jim Husbeth I'm trying to reach. But let me tell you his story." So I began going through the same narrative I had told the masseuse at my fitness club.

The man on the other end of the line listened intently, without interrupting, until I got to the part where I was crawling over beside him during the ambush and began praying the Lord's Prayer. He interrupted me and said, "No sir, it was the 23rd Psalm."

I was stunned and amazed! Thirty years had gone by. Two men had had a casual conversation on the back of a navy ship, then ended up in battle together before going their separate ways. Thirty years later another man's curiosity about a scar had brought those two men back in touch. Mere coincidence? Hardly! This was a God-thing. Once again, God was directing our steps.

Well, I just had to ask, "Hey, Jim, whatever happened to you when you got back? Did you ever make that decision about trusting Christ personally? Or are you still thinking about it?"

He told me, "Well, I guess you'd have to say I'm still thinking about it. After the medics delivered me to the aid ship, I found that a chaplain had placed a New Testament in my pocket. I've read through it some, and it's really helped me during some times of great pain and anguish."

We talked for a while. I could see he still had a lot of questions. I told him about my book, *Is Jesus God?* I asked, if I sent him a copy, would he read it?

"I'll call you the day I get it," he replied.

He was as good as his word. I sent off a copy of the book, and a few days later he called to say he had just finished reading it. I asked him whether what I had written made sense, and if so, whether he'd like to receive Christ. He replied, "I've just prayed the prayer in the back of the book where it explains how to receive Jesus as your Savior."

Thirty years after his first encounter with the gospel, Jim Husbeth had finally trusted Christ! He was so excited. "I have to come down to Texas and see you," he said enthusiastically.

I told him I was getting ready to go to Europe in a couple of days. But he was insistent that he come right away. So his wife drove him all the way to Dallas. During his visit, I enjoyed a marvelous, marvelous reunion with my fellow Marine, who was now my new brother in Christ.

God's clock and our clocks are never the same. Who knows why it took thirty years for the seeds of the gospel to take root in Jim Husbeth heart? Only God can know for sure. But He doesn't owe us any explanation. He simply promises us that: "My word. . .which goes forth from My mouth. . . will not return to Me empty, without accomplishing what I desire, and without succeeding in the matter for which I sent it" (Isaiah 55:11).

Confident, then, in both *the what* and the *when* of God's leading, we can walk by faith. We can *trust* that God is using everything—regardless of what it looks and feels like in terms of the circumstances—to bring about His glory and our highest good.

Andrew Murray put it better than I can when he wrote:

First: He brought me here, it is by His will I am in this strait place; in that I will rest.

Next: He will keep me here in His love, and give me grace in this trial to behave as His child.

Then: He will make the trial a blessing, teaching me the lessons He intended me to learn, and working in me the grace He means to bestow.

Last: In His good time, He can bring me out again—how and when, He knows.

Say: I am *here*—by God's appointment, in His keeping, under His training, for His time.

Endnote

[1] Quoted by V. Raymond Edman, *They Found the Secret* (Grand Rapids: Zondervan, 1984).

Chapter 22

COURAGEOUS TRUST

"Give me one man with courage and I will have a majority."
— Thomas Jefferson

I talk a lot about courage, but courage is largely a matter of pressing on when the circumstances around you and the feelings inside you are telling you to stay put. As Winston Churchill is said to have observed, "Success is not final, failure is not fatal: it is the courage to continue that counts." It takes courage to follow Christ because He's constantly desiring us to leave our comfort zones.

Think of the disciples on the Sea of Galilee, in a storm in the middle of the night. As they struggle with their boat, Jesus comes walking to them on the water. Imagining Him to be a ghost, they begin crying out in terror. But what does Jesus say to them? "Take *courage*, it is I; do not be afraid" (Matthew 14: 2 7, emphasis added). How often we need to hear the Lord's voice above all the shrieking winds of our own storms and struggles. He might communicate: *It is I, the One who loves you! Take courage! Trust Me! Quit living in fear!*

Peter does trust Jesus. And to prove Peter's trust, Jesus invites him to get out of the boat and walk on the water toward Him. Can you imagine how the Lord must have felt to see Peter straddle the side of the boat, put his feet down on the water, and then begin to walk! Using sanctified imagination, we can almost hear Him exclaiming: *That's it! That's it! You've got it, Peter! Way to go, buddy! You're trusting Me! Fantastic! Thank you, Peter! Thank you! See that, guys? That's faith! That's what I've been waiting for!*

As with most of us today, Peter's trust was short-lived. But the point is, God's best for us always involves getting out of the boat. There are countless boats that people flounder about in. It may be the boat of comfort and convenience. Or the boat of financial security. Or the boat of position and prestige. Or the boat of our own narrow-minded prejudices and presuppositions. Jesus challenges us to take courage and get out of our boat and walk toward Him, by His grace and in His strength. In doing so, we always experience God's best for our lives—with Jesus, out of the boat.

Jesus invites us to take risks. He challenges us to courageously trust Him and go against the circumstances and our own fears with the simple attitude, "Lord, I don't care what Your will is, I just know I want to be in Your will— no matter what."

I'm Alive Because of the Sacrifice and Courage of Others

If that seems like leaving ourselves open to self-sacrifice, it is. As G. K. Chesterton observed:

Courage is almost a contradiction in terms. It means a strong desire to live taking the form of a readiness to die. "He that will lose his life, the same shall save it," is not a piece of mysticism for saints and heroes. . . This paradox is the whole principle of courage; even of quite earthly or quite brutal courage. . . .

A soldier surrounded by enemies, if he is to cut his way out, needs to combine a strong desire for living with a strange carelessness about dying. He must not merely cling to life, for then he will be a coward, and will not escape. He must not merely wait for death, for then he will be a suicide, and will not escape. He must seek his life in a spirit of furious indifference to it; he must desire life like water and yet drink death like wine.[1]

I am alive today because of two men who sacrificially and courageously "drank death like wine" on my behalf. One of them was Sergeant Peter S. Connor, a member of my unit in Vietnam. One of our frequent missions in the war involved "search and destroy" of the many tunnels from which the Vietcong operated. In addition to using them for ambushes and escape, the enemy would booby-trap those tunnels with explosives. So, before sending our guys into a tunnel to check it out, we would clear it by throwing a hand grenade inside of it.

A hand grenade has a pin that holds down a spoon attached to a timed fuse. When you are ready to set off the grenade, you put your thumb over the spoon and pull the pin. As soon as you throw the grenade, the spoon releases, which pops the fuse, and in four or five seconds the explosive goes off.

One day as we were clearing tunnels, we found our grenades were exploding in two or three seconds instead of four or five. When I learned about that, I pulled our guys together and said, "Men, we've got a batch of faulty grenades here. So be very, very careful when you throw these things. Make sure you hold down the spoon right until you release it."

RADICAL TRUST

We resumed our work. A short time later, Sergeant Connor pulled a pin on one of the grenades while holding down the safety spoon, but this time the grenade triggered even before the spoon released. He only had a split second to react. The natural thing would have been to save himself by tossing the grenade away. Had he done so, it would have landed right in the middle of our unit. Instead, Sergeant Connor cradled the grenade on the ground between his arm and his leg. The explosion blew his arm completely away and did major damage to his leg.

A split second. The decision of a lifetime. One courageous man choosing self-sacrifice in order to save others.

We tried to stop the bleeding as best we could. Finally a chopper showed up, and the medics took Sergeant Connor out to a hospital ship. We all hoped and prayed for his life. Initially we were told he would make it. But a couple of days later we were informed he had died.

As his officer, I was in a position to recommend Sergeant Connor for the Medal of Honor, which is the highest military decoration a member of the armed forces can receive. The honor is given to a soldier who distinguishes himself or herself "conspicuously by gallantry and intrepidity at the risk of his or her life above and beyond the call of duty while engaged in an action against an enemy of the United States." After I returned from Vietnam to recuperate from my own wound, I was privileged to escort Sergeant Connor's wife and daughter to a Rose Garden ceremony at The White House, where President Lyndon Johnson presented Mrs. Connor with her husband's Medal of Honor.

Sergeant Connor died for me, his captain, and for all of the men in our unit, who were his comrades and friends. We had trained together, laughed together, and fought together. We trusted him; and he trusted us. We would do whatever was necessary to protect one another. Such loyalty and commitment was our pledge and our bond. As the officer of the unit, my job was to look out for the welfare of my men; Sergeant Connor's job was to execute my orders. And then came that moment when that brave man's loyalty was tested: Would he indeed lay down his life for me and the rest of the unit?

He made the ultimate sacrifice that definitely went beyond the call of duty. His choice displayed the courage that Chesterton described as "seeking his life in a spirit of furious indifference to it."

The Highest Honor That Will Ever Be Given

The other man who saved my life was even more courageous than Sergeant Connor. His name is Jesus Christ. I've already described the self-sacrifice He made on the cross. His death on the cross is the greatest act of courage the world will ever know. But the thing I come back to again and again is He made that sacrifice for *me*. He fully accepted the wrath of God poured out on *my* sin so *I* might experience the love of God forever. With His dying breath, Jesus was telling me: *John, I love you! Trust Me!*

When I ponder His great love, all I can say is, "Yes, Jesus, I trust You—no matter what!" And with the apostle Paul I declare, "I have been crucified with Christ; and it is no longer I who live, but Christ lives in me; and the life which I now live in the flesh I live by faith [that is, with full trust] in the Son of God, who loved me and gave Himself up for me" (Galatians 2:20).

Jesus gave Himself up for you and for me! No wonder He, too, will receive honor—the highest honor and the greatest glory that all of heaven and earth will ever muster:

> For this reason also, God highly exalted [Jesus], and bestowed on Him the name which is above every name, so that at the name of Jesus every knee will bow, of those who are in heaven and on earth and under the earth, and that every tongue will confess that Jesus Christ is Lord, to the glory of God the Father. (Philippians 2:9–11)

The One who loves us is the Lord of glory. The only meaningful response we can make is to fall at His feet and say, "Here, Lord, is my life.

Do with it what You will. All I want is You." When we get to that point, Jesus becomes our chief treasure. And when Jesus has become our chief treasure, then we really will believe "that to die is gain" (Philippians 1:21).

May our God and Father continue to open the eyes of our hearts to see the fullness of His beloved Son, for the sake of the glory of our Lord and Savior, as we live unto Him through Him and for Him.

Endnote

[1] G. K. Chesterton, *Orthodoxy* (Chicago: Moody Publishers, 2009), 91-92.

APPENDIX

You, Too, Can Have a Personal Relationship with God

I've talked in this book about my own relationship with God. There is nothing else in my life that has proven more valuable, more important, or more satisfying. But having read my story, you may be thinking, *It's great that John feels so connected to God. It really is. I sure don't have a relationship with God like John's. I don't feel at all connected to God. But I'd like to.*

You can! You, too, can have a personal relationship with God. In fact, that's exactly what God longs for—to know you intimately and personally, and for you to know Him intimately and personally. He's not interested in you following a religion; He wants a *relationship*—with you! Indeed, with every person.

So how does such a relationship occur? Perhaps the place to begin is to get clear on why none of us starts out with a relationship with God in the first place.

Think about one of your friends with whom you're really close. Now imagine that you do something so terrible that it destroys that relationship beyond repair. That's essentially the situation we find ourselves in with God. We humans have done something so terrible that it has irreparably shattered our relationship with God.

The Bible tells us what that terrible something is: "All [humans] have *sinned* and fall short of the glory of God" (Romans 3:23, NIV, emphasis added). I know that *sin* has become a politically incorrect word nowadays, but I'm not sure why. The term literally means "to miss the mark, to err, to wander off the path." I can relate to that, because I don't always live up to the standards of moral justice and righteousness that I set for myself. So why should I be surprised when a Holy God declares me to be a sinner because I've never come close to meeting His standard of moral perfection?

What is true of me is true of every human being: We are *all* sinners in the sight of God:

> The LORD looks down from heaven
>> on all mankind
> to see if there are any who understand,
>> any who seek God.
> All have turned away, all have become corrupt;
>> there is no one who does good,
>> not even one. (Psalm 14:2–3, NIV)

This is God's perspective from heaven. It's a pretty troubling assessment. Ironically, almost everyone on earth actually agrees with that assessment. The vast majority of people in the world say they believe in some form of a god or gods, but almost all of them believe something inside of them is broken in their dealings with that god. Indeed, almost all the religions in the world are about humans trying to find a way to connect with their god(s). All of those religions but one put the burden on humans to make that connection. If you pray certain prayers, observe certain rituals, avoid certain practices, and get everything just right, then maybe—just maybe—you'll get back into a good situation with your god. Many people in the United States believe that: do good, clean up your life, don't do anything really bad, and God *might* be open to accepting you.

If that's what you believe, then I have to tell you plainly that you're not a Christian, because that's not what Christianity teaches. Christianity is not a self-help program. It's not do-goodism. Doing good is commendable, but it's not enough to get us out of the ditch with God. In fact, do you know how God regards the efforts of sinners to justify themselves before Him on the strength of their own good deeds? The prophet Isaiah tells us:

Behold, You were angry, for we sinned,
We continued in them [that is, in our sins] a long time;
And shall we be saved?
For all of us have become like one who is unclean,
And *all our righteous deeds are like a filthy garment.*

Isaiah 64:5-6 (emphasis added)

Yet again, that's a pretty dire assessment of humanity's brokenness!

Becoming Clean Enough for God

Just imagine that your daughter is getting married. A week before the wedding one of the invited guests goes on a hunting expedition. He's a real man's man, so he and his buddies spend the whole week out in the wild. They sweat like pigs. They lie in the dirt. They slop through mud. They get all lathered up with camo paint and deer scent. And they go the whole week without taking a bath, or even brushing their teeth. It's a great male-bonding time!

Then, on the day of the wedding, the group of hunters heads home. The hour is late, and there's no time for the invited guest to go home and clean up. So he pulls into a filling station and goes into the men's room to wash his hands, throw some water on his face, and comb his hair. With that, he heads to the wedding.

He arrives late. In fact, the wedding ceremony itself is over and the reception has begun. But he walks in anyway—his body reeking, his breath foul, and his clothes just filthy. Yet he's quite confident of himself—so much so that the first thing he does is walk straight to the bride and give her a great big hug. How would you react? I think most any father would grab the guy by the arm and see him to the door.

But imagine that as you are leading him away he says, "Hey, man, what's wrong? I don't understand! I wanted to be part of the festivities, so I cleaned myself up as best as I could. Is that not good enough?"

RADICAL TRUST

Of course it's not enough! The man's intentions may have been good, but his actions have fallen short of the social expectations required for a wedding.

So it is with any attempts we make to *clean* ourselves up for God. Our efforts may be well intended, but they fall short (and remember, falling short is what sin is all about) of the spiritual expectations required for pleasing a Holy God.

Nothing we do as humans will ever be good enough to get ourselves out of the ditch with God. *Nothing!*

We have a serious problem. Because one of the reasons God is good is that He is just. And of course we *want* Him to be just. We don't want a God who turns a blind eye at wrongdoing, or lets people "get away" with murder (and other bad stuff), or tips the scales if someone buys Him off. No, we want a God who *is* truly just. And God is truly just—perfectly just. But that means He can have no tolerance for sinful, broken people, people who have fallen short of His standard. His justice must be satisfied. He can't just "let us off." If He did, He wouldn't be just.

Ironically, this presents God Himself with something of a dilemma (at least, from the human perspective). It's as if God holds a conversation with Himself in heaven and might say, "What am I going to do about humanity's sin and brokenness? That sin and brokenness have led to a separation between them and Me. My holiness demands justice, and what they justly deserve is to remain separated from Me. And yet I love every one of them beyond words. My love is so great that it cannot allow that separation to remain in place."

And then God might ask: "Who can satisfy the justice that I demand, in order to remove that separation and allow human beings the opportunity to experience the richness of My eternal love for them?"

And this is where real Christianity offers you and me some incredibly good news. It reveals that the God of the universe—who has a love that none of us can even imagine for all of us who are in the ditch—has said, in effect, and I paraphrase: "Here's what I will do. I'm going to come down into the ditch with you and deal with your brokenness and your sin. You can't get out of the ditch on your own, but I'm going to provide a way out. And if you will trust Me for your problem, I will not only get you out of the ditch, I will forgive you for all that you need to be forgiven of as it relates to your brokenness with Me. In fact, I will give you a life that you never could have imagined, and that life will last forever."

In Jesus Christ, God came down into the ditch with us and provided the way out of the ditch. When Jesus became a man and allowed Himself to be nailed to the cross, He satisfied God's justice. He paid the penalty for your sin and my sin that keeps us separated from God. He was able to do that because He had no sin Himself. He was perfect in His relationship with God the Father. But He took our sin upon Himself and paid the debt demanded by God's holy and righteous justice.

Jesus Paid the Debt and Conquered Death

What Jesus did is a bit like someone who has a friend with cancer saying to the doctor, "Listen, I know this innovative way to take all of the cancer cells out of my friend here and put them into me. Even though it will kill me, but it will allow my friend to live." Such a sacrifice would take an amazing amount of love for someone to do. But that's exactly what Jesus did for us. When He died on the cross, He took our "disease" of sin into His body so that we could become disease-free, sin-free, and live. He died in our place so that we might live. He did so out of His amazing love.

Of course, Jesus didn't stay dead. He was killed on a Friday afternoon, but on Sunday morning, He burst out of the tomb they had put Him in and began appearing to people. His resurrection showed that He had not only conquered sin, but He had conquered death, as well. So when He told one of His followers, "I am the resurrection and the life; the one who believes in me will live, even though they die" (John 11:25, NIV), He was speaking the truth. He had the power and authority to say such a profound truth. Later, for this reason Paul could write: "The wages of sin is death, but the gift of God is eternal life in Christ Jesus our Lord" (Romans 6:23, NIV).

God offers you and me a free gift: forgiveness of our sins (because Jesus paid the penalty on our behalf), restoration of our relationship with God (because now that our sins are forgiven, nothing separates us from God's boundless love), and eternal life (because Jesus' resurrection broke the power of death).

Earlier I stated, you *can* have a relationship with God. He longs to know you intimately and personally.

So how does that relationship take place? As I said, it's a free gift. But anything that is free must be received. The way to receive God's free gift is to believe it—to take God at His word by telling Him you accept His gift and want to enter into the restored relationship He offers you.

True Belief

Don't get tripped up over the word *believe*. It can mean a couple of different things. If I asked you whether you "believe" in George Washington, you would probably say, "Yes," meaning that you are satisfied in your mind that he was a man who lived in the eighteenth century and was the first President of the United States. You believe the facts about his life to be true because of the historical accounts of his life.

But now, suppose I asked whether you "believe" in your parents. Once again, you would say, "Yes," but this time you would not mean that you believe *about* them, but that you believe *in* them, and hopefully that you trust them and have faith in them, as well. It would be an experiential belief, the kind that cultivates true relationship.

God asks us to believe *in* Him because He is a real Person who desires a real relationship. He is asking us to trust in Him, rely on Him, and depend on Him to save us from our sins. When the Bible tells us to "believe in the Lord Jesus Christ, and you will be saved" (Acts 16:31, NIV), it doesn't mean to just believe that Jesus existed, or to accept certain doctrines about Him. It means to trust Him (and Him alone) as the One who has paid our penalty, brought about forgiveness, and provided the basis for a restored relationship with God forever. As John put it in his gospel, "These [that is, the words, miracles, and other things that John recorded about Jesus] are written that you may *believe* that Jesus is the Messiah, the Son of God, and that by *believing* [trusting *in* Him] you may have life in his name" (20:31, NIV, emphasis added).

Would you like to put your trust in Jesus right now, so that can you know without a doubt that you are right with God and in a fully restored relationship with Him? If so, let me suggest a simple prayer for you to express that desire to Jesus:

> Lord Jesus, thank You for loving me. I believe You died in my place so that I might be forgiven of my sins and have a fully restored relationship with God. Thank You for conquering death by Your resurrection so that I might receive the free gift of eternal life. I open my heart to You, and I invite You to be my Lord and my Savior. Thank You, Lord Jesus, for forgiving my sins and giving me eternal life. I ask You to make me the person You want me to be.

Think about that prayer. You are saying that you believe in what happened 2,000 years ago, that the God-Man Jesus came and died and rose again from the grave, as a historical fact. For the world, yes, but personally "for you," and you desire to receive this free gift of God that involves forgiving your personal sins and gives you the gift of eternal life. For Jesus Christ to do His part, God is asking you to trust in His love for you and ask Christ to be your personal Savior and Lord.

May I suggest that you receive this free gift and become a child of God? Look back and pray this prayer of personal belief in Jesus Christ.

RADICAL TRUST

After You Say "Yes" to Jesus

If you prayed that prayer to the Lord and meant it as a true desire of your heart, then let me assure you that God has heard your prayer, and you now have a new relationship with Him, and always will. As God's own Word promises, "To all who receive him [Jesus], to those who believed in his name, he gave the right to become children of God" (John 1:12, NIV).

And, remember you are not trusting in a prayer to save you, but you are placing your trust in a Person, the Lord Jesus Christ, to save you.

For futher information about your new relathionship with Jesus Christ contact East West Ministries for a free copy of the booklet *Is Jesus God* by John Maisel.

ABOUT THE AUTHOR

John Maisel has had a diverse background in various business and ministries activities since being honorably discharged as a captain from the U.S. Marine Corps in 1967. While in the Marine Corps he was awarded the Bronze Star and Purple Heart as a result of his tour in Vietnam. Before his time in the Marine Corps, John attended Oklahoma State University (OSU) where he majored in Business and Philosophy. As a scholarship athlete in football, John played quarterback and defensive back for the OSU Cowboys. After his senior year he was signed by the Houston Oilers where he failed to make the season roster as a defensive back.

RADICAL TRUST

After returning to Dallas in 1967, John desired to use business as a means of self-support for his Christian ministry to athletes and businessmen in Dallas and around the country. His business soon became a platform for his ministry to various business organizations and universities around the globe.

In 1982, Eastern European Seminary was formed where John became President and began to engage in full-time ministry behind the Iron Curtain. Eastern European Seminary was the first organization for what was later called Biblical Education by Extension International, headed by a consortium of organizations under Dr. Jody Dillow out of Vienna, Austria. When the Iron Curtain fell, John resigned as President in 1993 to form the present organization called East–West Ministries International. East–West was formed to penetrate closed countries that remained hostile to the gospel, classified as restricted access nations. Presently East–West engages in church planting and evangelistic outreaches in over twenty-five countries.

East–West Ministries Mission Statement: East–West Ministries International exists to evangelize and equip nationals to establish grace-oriented churches.

John stepped down in June of 2010 as President and CEO. He presently holds the title of Founder, Emeritus.

EAST-WEST MINISTRIES INTERNATIONAL

Throughout the 1980s, John Maisel traveled extensively behind the Iron Curtain to clandestinely train pastors and church leaders through an organization called Eastern European Seminary, later know as Biblical Education by Extension International (BEE). BEE had been the code name that became known throughout Eastern Europe and the Soviet Union before the formal name of EES was created. This original work was an inter-mission effort that had been led by Dr. Jody Dillow with headquarters in Vienna, Austria. When the Soviet Union and other communist governments collapsed in the early 1990s, the fruit of those efforts became evident when some 4,000 to 5,000 students were identified among the different levels of BEE training.

In 1992, John and others helped plant a church in Moscow and developed a partnership with an American "sister church" to help that new congregation mature. This development led John to transition out of BEE where he had served as President of Eastern European Seminary to form East–West Ministries International in 1993. As evangelistic opportunities began to develop, a dire need for trained church planters and pastors and new churches in the former communist countries began to explode as a spiritual harvest and openness to the gospel took place. The severely restricted Christian activity during seventy years of communist atheism began to see a new wave of the love of God as people moved from darkness to the light of Jesus Christ.

RADICAL TRUST

Today, East–West's mission remains the same: to evangelize, equip, and mentor faithful and reliable national pastors who will plant grace-oriented churches that will shepherd and disciple new believers and, in turn, plant more churches.

In 2002, John challenged East-West to a set of ten-year goals that he called The One Percent Factor: that God would use East–West to impact one percent of the five billion people in the world who had never heard the gospel or were indifferent to the gospel. The ambitious target was to train 10,000 Christian leaders, plant 1,000 grace-oriented churches, penetrate a hundred unreached people groups, and expose 50 million people to the truth of the gospel. By 2010, all of those goals had been met and exceeded, with the exception of reaching all 50 million people with the gospel. That work continues feverishly as East–West pushes toward achieving the ten-year benchmark in early 2012. As of 2010 East–West had exposed over thirty-seven million people to a clear presentation of the gospel in their own language.

In June of 2010, John and the Board named Dr. Kurt Nelson as President and Chief Executive Officer of East–West, and John assumed the title of Founder and Chairman of the Board Emeritus. Formerly, Kurt served as the Executive Vice President of Field Ministries since 1997. He is a career missionary with deep field experience in Russia, Asia and the Caribbean, along with countless engagements throughout Africa, India, and the former Soviet countries.

Kurt, John, and the entire team at East–West invite you to join them in the exciting work that God is doing through East-West all around the world. Opportunities for participation include:

- Praying for particular regions and ministry projects by signing up to receive weekly devotionals by John, newsletters, and ministry updates that communicate specific prayer needs.
- Going on a short-term mission trip with East-West to spread the gospel throughout the world.

For more information, visit East–West online at **www.eastwest.org**. Or contact us at:

East-West Ministries International
2001 W. Plano Parkway
Suite 3000
Plano, Texas 75075
972.941.4500

Follow on Twitter: @ewmi
Facebook: ewministries
Blog: ewmi.wordpress.com